YOUTH GROUP TRAVEL

A Planner's Guide

by Larry and Mary Kay French

Team Seattle

No Whiners No Prima Donnas

...and a ton of fun!

REEDSWAIN PUBLISHING

Library of Congress
Cataloging in Publication Data

by Larry and Mary Kay French
   Youth Group Travel
   A Planner's Guide

ISBN No. 1 59164 100 4
Library of Congress Control Number: 2005930239

Cover Design
Bryan R. Beaver

Cover Photo by
© Marian Cottrell

Printed by
DATA REPRODUCTIONS
Auburn, Michigan

Reedswain Publishing
562 Ridge Road
Spring City, PA 19475
800.331.5191
www.reedswain.com
info@reedswain.com

Introduction

What can this book do for YOU?

The purpose of this book is to aid you in organizing travel for groups of young people. Our experience has been in organizing travel for soccer teams. However, we feel that much of what we have learned applies to all youth travel groups. Exposing young people to travel opportunities tests their comfort zones, strengthens their self–confidence and builds new friendships, all of which helps them develop into well–rounded adults.

In the text, we will use the word "coach" to refer to the coach of any travel team. "Coach" can translate to bandleader, DECA counselor, gymnastics trainer or other leader. Likewise, realize that "player" may translate to student, gymnast or any youth group traveler. We've supplemented the text with stories from our travel with youth groups. The stories can easily be identified by the borders around them.

This book was designed to be a handy reference tool to help you simplify your planning process. If you have further questions, you can contact us through our website at www.teamseattle.info. We would be happy to help.

Make sure that YOU get to enjoy the group in whatever capacity that you fill. Sharing this experience before, during and after the adventure is truly a joy not to be missed.

Larry and Mary Kay French,

Team Seattle

Dedication

As corny as dedications are, this one is straight from the heart. Thanks to each of the hundreds of youth players that have shared these trips with us. You are our reason for continuing.

Acknowledgements

The travel opportunities that my family and I have experienced that led to this book have been an unbelievable gift. The support of friends old and new kept us motivated, but most of all, it has been the kids that have kept us coming back for more. Their teenage enthusiasm, their joy of discovery and their new-found confidence have been a reward beyond description. To share in this, even with all the hours of work and planning, has been priceless.

The willing teamwork and love from my better half, my wife and co-author, Mary Kay, were endless and fueled me to continue. The joy of growing up with our two fine sons, Brent and Adam, has kept me young and allowed me to never grow up. Our parents, Betty, Clay, Nori and Jim, implanted the work ethic and "can do" mentality.

A list of friends to thank would take a book in itself, but the interest and support from travel friends Claire and Terry Conway, Lisa and Bruce Kerr, and Vicki and Jack Goodwin supplied more ideas and new direction to expand our Team Seattle with each trip.

We frequently mention in this book that having a good rapport with your tour agent is vital. We have been blessed with more than good advice and have developed true friendships with our friends Joann and Loek van Zijl of Euro-Sportring Inc. and their qualified team around the US and Europe.

Lastly, we want to acknowledge our editor/book designer and good friend, Doug Jones, who's patience and talent got these words onto the paper with style and humor, the latter being one of his greatest attributes.

Table of Contents

Appendices Section

Chapter 1
The Game Plan

Itinerary

All Work and No Play...

One of your motivations for organizing a trip like this is probably your desire to expose your own son or daughter to new and interesting people and places...likewise for other family members, players, coaches and boosters. But in planning where to go, be a little selfish. There are opportunities to play great soccer, baseball or music, meet wonderful people and see spectacular sites throughout the United States and around the world. Where would you like to go?

In looking ahead at your initial meeting with the coach and then the parents, you must have this part of the package complete. Each person will have her or his own preferences, and if you open the choices up to everyone, your trip will die in committee. Getting input from your family, and only one or two other people is a good idea. It helps you test your philosophy and logic in preparation for those future meetings.

Here is a sample itinerary from a trip we took to the Italy Cup:

Team Seattle Itinerary
Spain/France/Italy Cup

120 Travelers—5 teams/68 players/5 Coaches
2 Group Leaders, 45 Boosters
Hotels: 1/Spain; 1/France; 2/Italy Cup
Busses: 2 @ 54 & 1 @ 24

LIASON

BUS | GUIDE

DATE	SITE/EVENT	BUS	LIASON	GUIDE	COMMENTS
June 25	Lv Seattle				
June 26	Arr Barcelona	√	√		Liaison at Customs
June 27	Tour Barcelona	√		√	+ 2 Friendly Games
June 28	Boat Tour in AM	√			Meet Bus in Blanes
	Blanes to Monserrat	√	√		+2 Friendly Games
June 29	Free Day				+1 Friendly Game
June 30	To Nice	√	√		
July 1	Tour St. Paul in AM	√	√		+ 2 Friendly Games
	Tour Cannes in PM	√	√		+1 Friendly Game
July 2	Day in Nice	√	√		+2 Friendly Games
July 3	Free Day				
July 4	To Cesenatico	√	√		
July 5	Tour San Marino	√		√	
July 6	Free Day		√	√	
July 7	Italy Cup Opening	?	√*		*Tournament Staff
July 8	Games	?	√		
July 9	Games	?	√		
July 10	Games	?	√		
July 11	Finals	?	√		
July 12	Depart from Bologna	√			

Below, is another example of our group's itinerary for a recent trip to the Holland Cup.

Team Seattle Itinerary
Chioggia, Italy/Amsterdam "Holland Cup"

52 Travelers/28 Players/2 Coaches/2 Leaders
20 Boosters/2 Teams, 1 Hotel each site/1 Bus

Day	Site/Event	Bus
Day 1 Mon	Leave SeaTac	
Day 2 Tue	Arrive Chioggia Via Venice Airport	Y
	Bus from Venice to Hotel La Bussola	Y
Day 3 Wed	To Venice by Public Bus/Boat	Y
Day 4 Thu	Morning tour Chioggia—Market Day?	
	Friendly Games	Y
Day 5 Fri	Free Day	
Day 6 Sat	Leave Italy – arrive Amsterdam	
	Stay at Casa 400	Y
Day 7 Sun	1/2 day Training + Zaanse Schanse	Y
Day 8 Mon	Sightseeing Amsterdam	
Day 9 Tue	Games	Y
Day 10 Wed	Games/Opening Ceremony	Y
Day 11 Thu	Games	Y
Day 12 Fri	Games	Y
Day 13 Sat	Holland Cup Close	Y
Day 14 Sun	Depart Amsterdam to Seattle	Y

When you get down to basics, it is not that different planning a group trip to Europe than to the opposite coast in the US. You still need to recruit people, move them, house and feed them, and keep them busy.

If you have traveled extensively, you have your favorites and know where you might like to head. If you haven't, evaluate what your preferences are. Do you like a hot place or a temperate one? Do you like the mountains, the seashore or the farmland? Do you like the cosmopolitan life or the country? Of course you take into consideration the needs of the group, but reward yourself with being in a location that excites **YOU**. It is one factor in keeping your motivation high throughout the trip.

In the chapter about travel and tour companies, there is more detail on what to expect from their services. One of these is to help you plan an itinerary that includes some of your favorites. If they know what your preferences and trip goals are in advance, they will be better able to put a custom trip together. Most of them have packages which may do fine. Don't hesitate to ask them to do special deviations for you. Depending on the situation, it may not be costly.

From my experiences and from interviewing other group leaders, a blend of games and performances, with time for sightseeing is important wherever you travel. Groups who hit one or more tournaments with tight schedules oftentimes found that they might as well have played and stayed at the other end of their hometown. They didn't get to "experience" the areas they'd visited. Even if you are aiming at the highest competitive level of play, you can still find time to see the area.

You can focus on one location, or two or more. Variety is one key to a successful trip. One bit of advice, though; remember that moving from place to place, packing and repacking, has the potential to raise the stress factor. The old seven countries in seven days is a surefire way to see the world through a camera lens out of a bus window, and to raise your blood pressure.

Two nights minimum at a stop is a good beginning. It allows everyone to settle in and scope out his or her new environs. Four to five nights are ideal if you are going to multiple locations. The travel days by plane, bus or train are basically shot. Spend as little of your time in that mode as possible.

I would suggest scheduling a tournament in one country or location which would probably eat up most of one week, and then a second country or location for fun and casual games for as long as your budget will allow. The order of this type of itinerary makes no difference, although the serious coach would rather hit the ground and play the "serious" competition while the players' attention is still on sports. A blend like this gives the trip more depth allowing for a greater experience for all. When you look back on the trip, you won't just have a single memory but a collection each with its own flavor. That's what life is about. It's more than just vanilla.

At each location, your travel company will provide you with facts about the area. It will help you a great deal to read up on the region ahead of time. There are thousands of travel books and videos where I have found little diamonds of information that I have asked to be built into my arrangements. And although the travel company will put an itinerary together for you, suggest changes. You are their customer.

Just as a mix of competition and travel can be successful, blending the sights that you visit is a definite plus. Very few groups will put up with a day of museums and cathedrals. But, as a part of seeing the area, it is important to mix your stops. You will be surprised what are on each persons top five favorites after a trip. Players won't just pick the water park any more than the boosters will only pick the flea market.

Whether or not the costs of side trips are included in your tour package needs to be defined before beginning the trip. This lets you and your entourage know not only how much extra money to bring, but should they want to relax and skip a tour, they need to know that prepaid tours are rarely refunded if individuals cancel.

Each group will have it's own personality. The leeway which you give to them in reference to independent "exploring" will vary. Turning players loose has a broad spectrum of possibilities, some of which are very good, and some have the potential of being bad.

The safety issue is always number one. Do you allow them to travel without adult supervision? The maturity level and locale are part of that answer. The younger the player, the less likely that you should grant her or him free roaming privileges. Also the larger the city, the less likely you are to allow it.

Traveling in groups of 3 or more is one of our most important safety rules. This photo shows some of the youth members exploring in Florence, Italy

Identify what your concerns are and discuss them with the group and their parents. This is an issue where consensus may reign. But even with older players, traveling in groups of three or more is a wise rule.

I do suggest that you immerse your group into the environment as soon as you land. Have an excursion to test the local bus or tram system. Have everyone begin to use the currency, and even the language if possible. This minimizes the chances that anyone is left just sitting in their room between group events like games, meals or tours. With your rules in place, encourage everyone to get out and see things. The trip will be over before they know it.

Team Philosophy

In an earlier section, I outlined my philosophy on how to select your itinerary. Now you must define **who** will go on the trip and develop your group philosophy, or code of behavior. Regardless of the gender, age or skill level of the players, it is critical to come to a consensus with them as to the rules of the road for the trip.

—Mutual Respect

As you will be in close quarters with this group (players, coaches, boosters), everyone must agree to show mutual respect to one another. There will always be disagreements, some of which will not be resolved, but it is acceptable to agree to disagree. Everyone is entitled to his or her opinion. In light that you had defined your objectives for this group at the initial meeting, there should be no surprises (although you may need to remind individuals periodically). In addition, establishing the group hierarchy and individual responsibilities will make it easier to settle disputes.

Make it clear that this respect and professional demeanor also applies towards opposing players and coaches, referees, and the staff of your transportation company, hotel, and tournament. As the group leader, be the benevolent dictator...and don't put up with whiners!

—Local Laws

Visiting different cities, states or countries means that you are now living under their laws. Simple things like chewing gum, spitting or littering may be much more serious there than at home. Do your research and listen to hints passed on by your booking agent and other travelers that you have accessed. In meetings with the group, inform the members of these unique codes by which they must agree to live or suffer the consequences. Shoplifting a small trinket may be very serious in a foreign country and may not only affect the individual, but also others in his or her company along with the group leader. When traveling to more than one area, these laws may change drastically, such as the approach to drugs in the Netherlands compared to Spain. Be very up–front with your members. This can turn a trip into a nightmare.

—Alcohol, Tobacco and Drugs

Involving the players in discussions of "team rules" will usually get the group to these topics quickly. Access to alcohol and tobacco is granted earlier in some states and countries. The impact of using these substances will affect a player's game and therefore will impact the team. The parents and guardians need to be consulted individually about any concerns and restrictions they might have on these subjects as they apply to their own sons or daughters. But *drugs* get you into trouble any way you look at it. Lay the cards out on the table and be straightforward about the consequences.

—Dating

Meeting people away from home can be a lot of fun. But good judgment, the area's laws, and your group's rules also govern this. Sneaking out at anytime to meet someone puts that individual as well as the group at risk. And what may seem as innocent at home may be taboo or a curfew violation in your host city.

—Tattoos and Body Piercing

Cities around the world offer these services to anyone with cash in hand. This is an area where parental consent will not be accepted. Team Seattle has a rule against getting a tattoo or a body piercing while on the trip. This is a health risk to our members because it is an unregulated industry. Sanitation standards are non-existent in many areas, so we "just say no" on this issue to all members.

Setting clear expectations in advance has helped our youth members learn the importance of being trustworthy, making our lives much less worrisome. These players are sightseeing on the streets of Nice, France.

Handling Members' Free Time

"Two's Company, Three is Better"

For the members to get the feel of an area, it is necessary for everyone to get away from the group to explore. But exploring can lead to unplanned situations. When alone, you have few options. With two in a group, your odds are up considerably. The best is to require that all exploring be pre–approved through the coach or guardian, and that everyone travel in groups of ***three*** or more.

Although this will not eliminate problems, your confrontations with pickpockets, thieves, pushy vendors, and occasional thugs are minimized with a group compared to a pair or a single. Because the group is traveling to see new sights, you need to plan for this exploration for all ages and genders. Again, with the sage advice from others, you can know what areas to make off limits.

When leaving the group, it is recommended that everyone notify another member of the group about their general destination and time frame. Players should have approval from the coach or their guardian in advance.

Making new friends is one of the perks of trips like these. Here the boys are bonding in Barcelona, Spain

Selecting Your Group Members

Or, No Whiners...No Prima Donnas

Selecting your group members is one of the major decisions that the group leader must make. If a team is the basis your travel group, then having enough players is key to playing competitively.

It may seem easier to take an entire pre–existing local team because of natural connections, such as the team your children are on. This, at first, may seem positive, and it may be. But think what "baggage" comes with that set group. It has been my experience that every team has a self–proclaimed star or two, and even worse are the "I don't want to coach but just to tell you how to run the team" type parents. Granted, in both cases, player or parent, you can usually work through things easily by communicating expectations **in advance**, but do you want to deal with this on the trip of a lifetime? I doubt it!

Your goals as far as level of success in competition also come into play at this point. Are you going on this trip to clean up and play to kill? Or, are you going to experience the cultures and peoples of the world? If the former is your focus, your team will have to reflect a much higher level of both commitment and of skill. With the latter, you have more flexibility to build a team based on compatible personality combinations. Seriously think about these factors. Do not rush through your selections. With careful planning, the trip can give you a lot of enjoyment, rather than grief.

A compatible group can make the trip into a much more rewarding experience for all. Pictured here is Team Seattle with a host team from Chioggia, Italy.

How do I exclude particular individuals from this travel group if I invite most other members of a team? Well, step back and once you have selected the age and gender, discuss with your coach or coaches other players who fit that group and fit the goals you have set. Our criteria have included our *"no whining, no prima donnas"* credo, plus we expect members to be flexible and supportive. **Don't** do a blanket invitation of just the one team. You limit your options and may not even have enough to make a travel team. The time, money and commitment may discourage more people than you thought. Broaden your base and invite many families. Set your criteria and be dead honest with yourself. From experience, don't make exceptions!

To introduce the selected families to your idea, I would suggest calling each family personally and letting them know that you are mailing them an invitation to a presentation of a great opportunity for their son/daughter. Don't go into too much detail on the phone. It will take you hours of phone calls if you have to repeat the details over and over again. Ask both the parents to attend if at all possible.

I have done this two ways:

1. The first way is having both the player and parent/s attend together. This is the easiest for you and cuts the number of orientation meetings in half.

2. The second way is having *only* parents attend the first meeting. This allows the parents to focus on the presentation, and also saves them a lot of grief if they immediately decide that this opportunity is **not** for them (Finances? Schedule conflict? General disinterest?). Unless you have the parents behind you, the youth members won't join.

The meetings themselves have an important purpose. You have the opportunity to watch for potential problem members. Look for people who over-criticize, monopolize conversations or who show a negative side that could escalate into problems later. On the positive side, the meetings may highlight individuals who can be valuable in many ways and can fuel some exciting hype within your team and community.

For your presentation, a combination of written material, video excerpts, and oral details have worked well. Be ready and professional. Do not waste their time. Dissatisfaction spreads like wildfire in a meeting of this nature. Have lots of maps on foam board, tour pamphlets, and other neat things to grab and look at. Having good snacks is another plus. A length of 90 minutes plus question time is plenty. Keep things on schedule and start on time. This is your first proof that you are a worthy and organized group leader.

At the end of this session, if you followed option # 2 on the last page, offer the next meeting time and date where the players are also invited. A period of two weeks is good. The object of the first presentation was to interest the parents. The second presentation is to focus on the players. Your materials and video may have to be altered to peak their interest. Plan for your "customer" and you will be successful. Fewer details are necessary at the second meeting. Do not ask for deposits at these first two meetings. At the close of this second meeting, present the date when you will begin taking deposits. If a family decides that they can live with the criteria, the itinerary and the costs, they need to be nudged into the commitment with this deposit schedule. Again, don't wait too long from this session. Keep the momentum going. Set the amount of the deposit based on how long you have before you actually leave on the trip, but set the amount enough to make the families think seriously before handing you the first check. I have asked for a $200 deposit at this point in the planning. Having people drop out is inevitable, but stressful.

With my travel teams, I began each initial orientation meeting letting each parent know that my priorities were for good, not killer, soccer to be combined with travel in spectacular places. There would be no tryouts. Each parent in the room represented a player that we wanted. My credo is simply: *No whiners and no prima donnas.*

I also told them that I was personally responsible for those families who were invited. As I had selected local coaches, I did not want there to be repercussions on them for players on their formal teams who, in my opinion, did not meet the group's criteria and, as mentioned above, were therefore not invited. If any parent wished to enquire if someone they would like to recommend had been considered, I encouraged them to call me. The burden was on them to prove that family met this no-whiners and no prima donnas credo.

In my orientations, I make it clear that we offer the opportunity
for family members to sign up and enjoy the fruits of the tour
as well. This plants the seed at the beginning of your planning.

I also planned for this to become a family trip, inviting parents, siblings and relatives, as long as they were also aware of our simple code. Our focus was on the players and our arrangements reflected it. If the boosters (defined on the next page) were not comfortable with the plan, they were politely told to consider a different trip on another occasion. The more honest and up–front that we were, the better the trip was. Spend even more time on those adults that you do not know well. And as you will see in other chapters of this book, **document everything**. Keep phone logs and put important conversations down on paper, copying affected persons. What you put off as minor at home becomes titanic when you are on the tour.

If you plan on taking more than one team, consider compatible age and gender groupings. Ask yourself if the itinerary that you have selected will be suitable for those groups individually. What if you are taking a boy's and a girl's team, or a group of 14 and 18 year–olds? Does this complicate your ability to be flexible once on the trip? Probably not, but consider what may surface. And ask your travel specialist. They have done this before and have seen it all.

A compatible group of young men and women
make the trip a pleasant experience.

Boosters

Love 'Em or Leave 'Em

The concept of traveling with lots of people may or may not appeal to you as the group leader. In a perfect world, if you did have the perfect group, every youth participant would be skilled, even-tempered, and flexible. The boosters (meaning anybody but the youth participants, such as parents, siblings, grandparents, club and city officials, and other friends) would be supportive, generous, and also flexible. But since our world is not perfect, step back again and think long and hard about this piece to your travel puzzle.

But, the old saying that "there is strength in numbers" does not necessarily apply to a travel project like this. It can be rewarding with a carefully picked entourage. It can also become the trip from hell.

If you are willing to aim for the sky, you can open your trip up to boosters. With the boosters, make it clear to them that the trip's emphasis is on the players' needs. This applies to the itinerary, transportation, and especially, the lodging and meals. My credo, "no whiners and no prima donnas," applies to boosters as well.

On the one hand, you can select a few adult boosters to help deal with herding your flock. This certainly minimizes your risk. Choose them carefully. Decide the areas where you need assistance and find individuals who have that ability. (See Chapter 8, *Division of Labor*) Are you looking for help with equipment and luggage, with in-trip transportation/meal/lodging arrangements, with discipline, etc?

It can be helpful having a few adults assist your flock of youth travelers. Above is the parade to the opening ceremony of the Italy Cup in Cesenatico.

Don't forget that it is invaluable having boosters along who might be nurses or doctors, who speak the language if you are abroad, who are good with a still or video camera, who are good at organizing impromptu parties, who are good at fundraising, or whose company matches funds for non-profit groups. This type of support is invaluable for you as the group leader.

In my experience, there is more potential for grief from the boosters than from the players. Most of the time, the players, rather than the adults, are more willing to be flexible when surprises pop up or when changes are needed.

Regardless of which road you take, make up your mind to be up-front with everyone from the beginning. Plan on changes and flexibility. If you can't envision being blunt with anyone in your group, think twice about taking them.

Mary Kay, Larry and coach Rich Borton

The "No Whining" tee shirts were a not-so-subtle reminder to the boosters on the Team Seattle trip to Holland and Spain in 1997.

Example: In Spain we stayed in a large hotel comparable to a six story Motel 6, but with tile floors. The facility was clean, included all the meals for hungry soccer players and had two pools. It was in peak season, 100°F by noon, and was filled with young people from all over Europe. It was noisy, but what kind of a hotel takes 34 soccer players (let alone the 53 boosters)? Complaints from 3 or 4 of the boosters: no bar soap or wash cloths in the rooms; no air conditioning in the rooms; and noise between 4:00–11 PM (until the discos opened) and again at about 3:30 am (when the discos closed). So you go to the store next door, buy soap for 30 cents, a washcloth for 70 cents and a fan for $7.00. The answer to the noise was to get into the swing of things and make our own noise. My wife and I proudly wore our "No Whining" tee shirts given us by our good friend and coach, Terry Conway. He liked our motto and his contribution helped us make our point at our daily briefing to our group.

Setting Your Budget

Unless you and your group are fortunate enough to have a sponsor, or you all have deep pockets, your total trip cost *does* matter. Variables like destination, length of stay and itinerary can easily inflate a budget to a level that is beyond the means of many families.

In your budgeting process, involve your trip banker or treasurer, and a few other key individuals like your coaches. Brainstorm a list of expenses such as:

1. Transportation (plane, bus, boat, van)

2. Lodging (hotel, dorm, boat, home-stay)

3. Food (meals that are included and those that are not)

4. Tours/excursions

5. Guides and interpreters

6. Uniforms

7. Equipment (if needed)

8. Tips

9. Gifts

10. Banking costs

11. Player scholarships and subsidies.

12. Meeting/party fund (room rental, guest speakers, door prizes)

13. Pre-trip site visits

14. Office expenses (copies, postage, faxes, phone line)

If you use a tour or travel company, their quote to you may include items like #'s 1–5 above. Tally these along with your guesstimates on the rest of your costs. This tally should yield a per–person cost. We suggest padding this by 5% to 10% to give you a buffer and a discretionary slush fund that may come in handy on the trip. The per–person cost for our 12 to 13–day European trips, from 1997 through 2002, averaged $2,200.00 to $2,500.00.

Sample Budgets

BUDGET # 1: Destination = San Diego from Seattle
Costs are Per Person
7 day Itinerary: Southern California

Transportation: Plane	**$ 210.00**
Rental Van: 1 Week/ 6 persons	**$ 30.00**
Van Fuel: 4 Tanks/6 persons	**$ 20.00**
Lodging: 4 persons/room X /6 nights	**$ 150.00**
Meals: 7 days X 3 meals/day	**$ 30.00**
Event Fee: (tournament, competition)	**$ 30.00**
Uniforms	**$ 45.00**
Tips	**$ 25.00**
Gift Chest	**$ 5.00**
Banking	**$ 2.00**
Slush Fund	**$ 50.00**
Office Costs	**$ 5.00**
Buffer	**$ 15.00**

Total per-person cost = $ 617.00

You may also work out a separate price for players whose costs may differ from that of boosters. Players need uniforms and pay a tournament fee whereas boosters do not. Players can usually be housed 3 or 4 to a room, but boosters are usually 2 to a room.

Another factor in budgeting is the number of people that your charter buses can hold. If they hold 50 and you have 56, you'll need two busses. This would double those transportation costs! In any case, you want your budget and per–person cost to be attractive to your target market.

The discretionary slush fund mentioned on the last page can be used to enhance various parts of your program. You can use it to pay for emergencies, meeting rooms, special tours, unique meals or additional supplies.

BUDGET # 2: Destination = Europe
Costs are Per Person:
14–day Itinerary: Italy and Holland
(Includes air, hotels, meals, bus transfers, tours, guides, event fees)

Tour Package Cost	**$2,784.00**
Uniforms	**$ 45.00**
Tips	**$ 25.00**
Gift Chest	**$ 10.00**
Banking Costs (checks, account fee)	**$ 2.00**
Slush Fund	**$ 50.00**
(Includes room rent for parties/meetings, guest speakers, door prizes, special meal or activity on trip)	
Scholarships	**$ 25.00**
Office Costs	**$ 5.00**
(Includes copies, postage, faxes, phone expenses, printer cartridges, printer paper)	
Buffer	**$ 100.00**

Total Per-Person Cost = $ 3,046.00

Food and Travel

Throughout this book we make mention of researching your destination, whether it be Texas or Italy. We also refer to food here and there as part of various activities. With our family's ties to the food service industry, and with our love of good food, we have given this category special priority during our planning phase, and it has proved to be a hit with our travelers, be they old or young. Of all the comments that we receive during and after our trips, a large percentage involve our members' new and positive experiences with the cuisine of the area.

We are aware that many people are not into food to this extent, but presenting some interesting facts about specialties of a region might entice them into trying something new. This is one of life's joys and makes one appreciate the differences within our nation and of our world. Nudging our group towards these new discoveries has always been rewarding.

Researching regional culinary treasures is very easy. As you find new sources of information about your destination, food will invariably be mentioned, as people are very proud and territorial about their recipes. As corny as it seems and as frequently as we all hear that recipes we passed down from generation to generation, it is true. Travel within the United States can offer just as wide a variety of taste treats as can other parts of the world. But in any case, we encourage you to highlight one or two items from your destination.

Some of these specialties may be different types of canned or bottled beverages common in one area but not available in your hometown. A great example of this is European Fanta, a soda pop with flavors not sold here in the USA. This is always a huge hit with our youth members. Another hit with the kids is the thin crust, Pizza Margarita (named for a queen who needed a little snack between lunch and dinner). You will see this everywhere in Europe. The local paellas of southern Spain, the pastas and gelati of Italy and the pancakes of the Netherlands are other examples. "Mahi and chips" from California or Hawaii, Creole delights of Louisiana, and the chowders of New England are American examples.

How do you get your members to try these? Well one way may be to inquire with your lodging management. They may already have some of these items included in your meals if provided. If not, ask it they can be added to the menu. There will be times when you are out as a group or as small groups and you will naturally fall into neighborhood food stands, café's and restaurants where the menus will be posted at the front. This also gives you a chance to scope out the prices as well. *Especially for the youth members, these times for exploration are really important to allow some time to be independent (with three or more in a group) and learn that they are capable of finding their way to and from sites, of ordering food and beverage in a different language, of using the local currency if different from ours, and of liking new food. It builds their self-confidence and has been one of our goals on all of our trips nationally and aboard.*

As we want to share with you and our past travel group members some of the great food that we have enjoyed, my wife and master chef, Mary Kay, has spent hours perfecting her version of many favorites. These recipes and the attached anecdotes may or may not help you in this project of planning a youth trip, but nonetheless, they are available in Appendix G. And don't be afraid to try these recipes, as this will broaden your horizons as well.

These players are going wild over fresh Pizza Margarita,
Caprese Salad and fresh, brick–oven baked bread.

The Pre–Trip Plan

Once you have gathered the ingredients for your group (once again, in our case the players, coaches, and boosters), it is necessary for the group to meet and mingle to create the best recipe for success. With an existing team, this is less of a challenge as you have had the regular season for this mixing to occur naturally. But for a "custom built" travel team, this is probably not the case.

For the players, it is necessary to evaluate and perhaps improve their fitness and skills. For everyone going, and their families, it is necessary to weave their varied personalities into a cohesive group. How can you do this? I have listed a few methods that I found were successful.

I. .... The Trip Kickoff Event

With the group mostly selected (you may be searching for more players), plan an indoor kickoff event. Invite all committed and probable players, coaches, boosters *and* their families. With the potential for this group being so large, select your location carefully. I suggest indoors as it keeps the group together in a somewhat confined area where they are more likely to meet and greet. This is the main focus of this event. The excitement and enthusiasm will escalate as the members and their families mix. Pick the location suitable for an activity where more mixing and mingling are required. Find a place where you can get a little noisy. I have found that a school cafeteria works well. The administrators of the school are usually more than willing to give you access if you explain that some of the players are students at that school.

Active games are a great ice breaker for the group.

—Activity

Plan an activity which is team–oriented, requires lots of activity to keep the group interested, and has multiple phases or stations. I have set up stations where small teams of 3 or 4 players rotate and compete for points in such activities as soccer bowling, header basketball, soccer golf, trapping tennis, Frisbee toss, plastic horseshoe toss, and geographic question sessions regarding your itinerary. Mix the players if you are taking more that one gender and age group. Give the teams funny names relating to the trip (Barcelona Bombers, Seattle Cup Sleuths). Have score sheets for each team. Have parents attend and run the stations, and calculate scores. Consider having each team use only 2 members at each activity station and rotate so that all members do several stations (similar to "best ball scramble" in golf). Schedule time to allow for a final round for the top 2 or 3 teams. We have set that round up like the "Family Feud" game show. Divide your audience into support groups and provide them with signs encouraging cheering and loud support.

Each player had to bring a $5+ item (CD, fast food certificate, teen gadgets, cash) to this event. These items were displayed, and at the end of the event, were distributed by final team score. The first place players each selected one gift, then the second place team, and so on. If someone forgot a gift, we got $5 in cash from the parent and added it to the gift display. We had no problems with this part of the program and it was a big incentive as some players brought gifts of over $5.

We even had a parent make reusable name tags for everyone involved. Even parents and siblings not going on the trip had name tags for these group events.

—Food

Make this a potluck. Have two or three of your families make the calls and ask for specific menu items (salad, hot entree, bread, dessert, beverages, paper goods). Put them in charge of set-up. Preplan the food location safely in a corner or away from the games. Having the meal at a specific time, followed by the games, and then the dessert will maximize the opportunity for the group to mingle with people that they just met during the games. See *Appendix G* for some all-time favorite recipes, like *taco soup, Crunchy Chicken Wings, Ugly Puffs and artichoke dip.*

—Trip Information

It is also a winner to wrap up the evening with one or two tidbits of new information about the trip, such as that you have arranged for a lunch at a castle, a boat excursion, a tour of a major stadium, or a meeting with a professional player. It sends everyone home with more fuel to keep their interest burning.

II.... Practices

Depending on the time of year that you are traveling, the players may be already active in practices with other teams or bands as well as other activities. The older the players, the greater the number of conflicts that will arise, such as jobs, dates and other responsibilities. Don't let this discourage you. Work out a schedule that is convenient for the coaches and players alike. Set a reasonable number of required practices out of the total number planned. For example, have the players attend at least three of six practices in a two–week period. If players are involved in other sports, they may be doing valuable conditioning with other coaches. Track, cross–country and basketball all give good workouts, but are not the only exercise options that work.

Work with the coaches on a basic program customized for each team. What are the strengths and weaknesses of the team? Where should you focus your training energy? Involve the players in the planning phase. The more–skilled players can be a great resource in helping other players in a proactive way.

III.. Local Tournaments and Competitions

Before leaving on your trip, you might want to "road test" the strengths and weaknesses of your tour group. This is one way to test their skills and give them an opportunity to spend more time together. Gauge the level of the tournament to where you realistically expect to be at tour time. It will not do much for the teams' self–esteem to get badly beaten. On the flip side though, it is important to provide them with a challenge.

Finding a local tournament has the advantage of less travel time, but a location requiring a hotel stay will really bring a group together. This is as important as the competitive play. If you do stay out of town, mix the players during room assignments. Put each with one good friend and one or two new faces. They might as well get used to such arrangements, as this will be the case on their trip.

Taking your travel group to a local tournament before the trip can be a great team-building exercise. Here players from one team cheer on our other team.

IV... Meetings

Relaying information to individuals and to families is one of your biggest challenges. In my experience, I have found it best whenever possible to do this in face–to–face group meetings. This minimizes misunderstandings from bad or incorrect interpretations from other people or from written information they might not understand. You will still rely on these latter two methods, but should attempt for these in–person opportunities whenever possible. Group meetings are the most time efficient.

Arrange your meetings for success. Pick dates in advance to allow people to plan their schedules. The frequency will depend on the amount of time before your trip. I found that meetings every other month work well. Set your agenda and try to keep the meetings to about an hour. It is difficult to process too much information at any one time. If group members have items for the agenda, make it known that they need to call a week early for your planning.

Start the meetings on time. Do not punish those who are on time while waiting for those who are delayed. You may have meetings that are more appropriate for just players or just parents. I have had such separate meetings running simultaneously in different parts of my home. Each meeting has it's own agenda, leader and focus.

I do like having these meetings in my home, as it is convenient for me and more personal for the members. Rooms in community centers, libraries, churches and schools are other possibilities. For some group members, this may be a big part of their social life, and you may have trouble getting the group to break up after the meeting. I usually advertise a starting and ending time allowing for a half hour of social time at the end. Those who wish to leave after the hour meeting can do so.

Be enthusiastic at your meetings! This is going to be the trip of a lifetime for the group. If you reflect the excitement, the members will follow suit. Have fun as you go!

Keep your members' attention by bringing visuals like maps, brochures and pictures mounted on foam board, or short videos of your destination

Rotate families who bring light snacks and beverages to the meetings. Do not make the food too elaborate unless you want everyone to stay all night. Punch or juice and cookies are all you need.

The agenda will vary depending on your group and the amount of time until you leave on your trip. As details come, they need to be presented. Guest speakers limited to a part of your meeting can add dimension to your travel destinations. It is a natural time to collect paperwork, but I do not encourage you to collect money at these events. You and your treasurer will have enough going on at these meetings.

After the meeting, I advise mailing or emailing out minutes to all families. For those families who did not attend, meet or call them to go over the minutes once received. To cut down on this, let everyone know that his or her attendance is expected (which sounds better than "required") at each meeting.

And remember; do not have a meeting just to have a meeting. Make the time count! People have enough going on without adding more unnecessary meetings to their schedule.

For your youth members, you need to help them visualize what it will be like when they are at the sites you'll visit. Then they'll get excited and be motivated to do their part to make the trip happen. Here, our son, Brent (r), explores Florence with friends Dale Tan and Matt Unseth.

Chapter 2

Sports Tour and Travel Companies

Even if you have traveled before, team travel has its own special and important requirements. Your local travel agent who normally handles your personal business or vacation arrangements may not have the expertise for team travel. There are specialized sport tour & travel companies that offer extensive options for your team travel experience.

For our first trip in 1997, I approached six different companies. I got their names from brochures I'd saved, and from the recommendations from other sports travel groups. I gave each some general parameters and requested bids, literature and four to six references. I then spent many evenings calling these references. We had our questions pre–planned.

Examples of questions included:

- What was that group's general itinerary? Two back–to–back tournaments? One touring week and one tournament?

- What did they like/not like about their general itinerary?

- Was the makeup of their group similar to our group? Players and a couple of coaches? Boosters too?

- What service did the company offer before the trip? During the trip? After the trip?

- Did the company meet or exceed their expectations?

- Did anything minor or major go wrong on their trip? How easily and quickly did it get resolved?

- What role did this person play in their trip? Coach? Manager? Player? Booster?

- How can we speak to others in that group?

- What would they have done differently/the same?

This investment of time up–front gave us many great ideas and new questions as well. We were better able to select our company with confidence. Over the years, we have developed a close relationship with our tour company, which has proved invaluable. We have made our preferences known to them, and they in turn have been able to make recommendations that fit our philosophy and our needs.

We have found it invaluable for the same company to have an office and agents in the areas we tour, and it is great to meet face–to–face with the hometown agent at least once during your pre–trip planning phase. It really connects you with them. A missing tour bus, for example, can more easily be remedied with a local call than to call 9 time zones away to another continent.

Once you have narrowed your choices on tour companies down to two or three, do more research on them. Reread their literature and list your questions. Check out their websites as well.

You should remember that *you* are the customer. Some sales people will try to sell you what is best for *their* company, or easiest for them as a sales representative. *You* are the boss! Be reasonable, but don't hesitate to ask even the simplest of questions. If they want your business, they will work for you.

I have had tour agents try to add in features that I could not afford and/or need:

1. ***Tour Guides and Liaisons.*** For exploring some areas, a trained guide is helpful. They know the area's history, flora and fauna and can suggest changes in your itinerary. They can be expensive, though. A liaison is usually also a local person who knows the area but doesn't have as much formal knowledge. A liaison, oftentimes a student, costs less, is a better fit for youth travel groups and knows the interesting everyday events of the community. Trust your judgment as to when you want some support for your group and when you do not. The assistance of such people may be worth it, but will increase your tour cost.

2. ***The Meal Package.*** Having three meals per day seems like a good deal, but remember if the group is away from the lodging, especially at midday, you need to return for the meal service. This may interrupt your performances, games and sightseeing. I usually steer the agent to **not** include "full board" (room and three meals per day), but they may try on behalf of the hotels to sell this. It needs to be *your* choice.

3. ***Featured Tours, Events or Tournaments.*** The sales staff of many tour companies are encouraged and rewarded for selling you **THEIR** tours, events or tournaments, some of which may not be destinations on your agenda. Be sure that you are getting the package that **you** want. Don't settle for what is best for the agent or company. They may have good suggestions for your consideration, but keep the ultimate decision making process within your small planning group.

Confirm the spectrum of the services that they can provide for your group. Do they book/arrange transportation, lodging, meals, hosts, tournaments, training sessions, specialty tours and guides? The more the travel company can do for your group, the less work for you. Do these services have additional cost? Of course they do, but your time is valuable, and when divided up among a group, it's oftentimes a bargain.

Document your phone conversations and print important emails for reference later. There are so many details that you should not attempt to remember everything. When you are getting quotes for the services you desire, get them in writing and double-check them for accuracy. Just like you and I, busy companies can make mistakes and they **will** refer back to any written documentation when issues arise if it helps *them*. It is also in *your* best interest to be able to refer them to the relevant documentation to help resolve problematic issues.

Surcharges

For pricing, ask if the price is fixed per-person, or as the group grows, are there free trips or price reduction levels (example 1—15 people = $1,500 pp; 16–25 people = $1,450 pp, etc.)? Depending on when you book, there can be surcharges for unforeseen increases in costs for lodging, flights, etc. I always agree on fixed prices knowing that we may overpay slightly depending on tourism trends and the economy. But this protects us from such extra surcharges that can decimate your budget buffer.

> I had a coach tell me of one tour company that came back to his group with last minute "surcharges." Upon questioning them, he was told that the cost of jet fuel had gone up so much that the airlines had increased their fares. That was true in part, but only for new bookings. Those reservations already ticketed were not affected and the agent was just trying to gouge the tour group.

On one occasion, the new Euro had strengthened against the US dollar, and the tour company sent the group a bill for this increase. Now if this was part of the original agreement, that should be expected and built into your budget, but if such surcharges come out of the blue, you should not just roll over and pay off. Fair is fair.

Our tour company has always been very clear on these issues in both printed material and in phone conversations. This reduces the opportunity for such distressing confrontations.

Is there a price available for a land-only package (hotels, meals, tournament, tours) if some members wish to arrange their own transportation? By using their frequent flyer miles, or for travel within North America, by driving their vehicle, some families cannot only send the player, but also other family members. Adding additional members may reduce the per-person package cost.

With all the money matters settled, discuss the payment plan with the tour company. It is not unusual for them to require a per-person deposit ($100–$200) when booking. Then, you need to find out what the payment schedule is. Monthly installments are the norm, but don't be afraid to ask for a special plan. I have, for example, requested that we make no payments to the tour company in January (post holidays) or April (tax time). This helps your members budget their payments to your treasurer. Final payments are often due 30 days before your departure. Also ask if your members can pay with credit cards. We have not been so lucky, but I have heard that some companies will agree to this.

Your tour company will have a cancellation and refund policy. We have had one last-minute cancellation (one to three people) on each trip we have planned. A traveler with a broken ankle or illness, a player making the Olympic Development Program (ODP) team, and an injury to a parent all surfaced within days of our departure dates. Plan for such unforeseen events by getting, in writing, your tour company's policy. Although you'll be dealing with the tour company, your team family involved in this dilemma will feel that it is *you* who are responsible for their refund. This can result in hard feelings with them and make future contact with them very uncomfortable.

Travel and trip cancellation insurance is offered by many tour companies. Their coverage varies widely. Some reimburse you a decreasing percentage as the trip gets closer, while others will refund the entire amount. Read all the fine print. Make the cost of this extra to your travelers, and if possible, have them enroll themselves, which takes you out of the middle.

If details of the policies of cancellation confuse you as they do me, delegate that research to someone in your group that is used to dealing with such fine print. When you are talking about losing hundreds to thousands of dollars if the need for a trip cancellation arises, the affected family will be very intense on the details and time frame. Do your homework and be prepared so as not to ruin the rest of your trip.

If you are using this tour company to book you into a tournament or training camp, make sure that your slot/s is guaranteed. Some companies organize their own tournaments and camps offering potential extra slots to other travel companies. One group that I interviewed was three weeks from departing when their agent notified them that they were being switched to a different tournament in a different country. That would be disaster in my mind and would also waste most of your groups' advanced geographic and historic research.

A tour company can make your trip a dream vacation to be remembered for a lifetime. Ours certainly has. But on the other hand, they can make it a nightmare. Do your homework.

Chapter 3

Tips on Selecting Your Airlines, Hotels, & Tours

Traveling with a group can be wonderful, but many of your trip planning decisions need to be made by keeping in mind the logistics of the size and make–up of your group. Large groups take longer checking in at airports and hotels, longer in boarding busses or trains, and longer in being fed a meal or touring a castle or stadium. Younger players require a greater ratio of chaperones to players. Adults are pickier about airline seating and hotel rooms. Young people are more concerned about liking the food and selecting a roommate. Thinking through these pieces to your puzzle will help you in the long run.

When working with a tour company, your package may or may not offer choices of airlines, hotels or tours. If you have any strong preferences, don't hesitate to discuss this point with them before they send you their proposal. It can't hurt to ask, and it saves them time in revising their proposal if you will be requesting options.

It may be an advantage to you and others in your group to fly on a carrier with whom you have a frequent flyer membership. Accruing mileage on this trip may provide you with more future travel opportunities. You can also recommend joining such a frequent flyer program to your other members.

"On the Road Again"

Getting there is more than half the battle!

Timing your departures/transfers/arrivals is also worthy of your attention. Knowing that there are probably a limited number of flights/trains/buses to your destination, I suggest that you list the possible problems as you see them. Considerations could include:

- Are your departure/trip dates on or near holidays or major events (graduation) that will be a disincentive for families to join your tour group? Also check out those holidays and events in your destination (Bastille Day in July, for example, is a bad day to arrive in or depart from France).

- Does your departure time put you at your destination at a difficult hour there? What problems could occur if you arrive/depart between 11:00 PM to 5:00 AM? Ground transportation issues like bus/train/ transfers may be a problem during those hours.

- Do you have layovers? Are they tolerable? Can you take advantage of sites there during the transfer? In Minneapolis/St Paul for example, the airport is just minutes by free shuttle to the Mall of the Americas.

If flying, you and your group can work out the procedure for getting seating assignments. Remember that it's very important to your young adults to sit with their friends, and for the guardians to sit near their charges. I have made groupings of 4 to 5 people and asked that the airline assign that group their seats in 2's, 3's, 4's or all 5 together. It has worked out well. Advanced planning of such a request allows the carrier to do this task in their free time.

Lodging Topics

A Pillow For Every Head

You should discuss your thoughts and preferences on lodging for your group with the key members. There are many options: home stays, dorms, or hotels. Since you know the make–up of your group better that anyone, you need to proceed with these arrangements with the whole group in mind. Youth groups tend to be high energy, and that means noise and activity. More guardians hopefully mean better control, but higher expectations. Your accommodations must match your group. Think of putting your group in the middle of a china shop. Are you setting yourself up for accidents, damages and stress?

And regardless of where you stay, talk to your members about security of their valuables. Passports, money, credit/debit cards, electronic gadgets and clothing are all subject to theft if not properly locked up. If the facility provides a safe or security storeroom, use it. Get the guardians involved in making this happen. It saves a lot of grief.

If you use a tour operator, they will be your conduits in matching your group into a suitable facility. It's their business.

Home Stays

Home on the Range

Home stays offer the chance to meet a local family and experience that culture up–front and personal. It does, however, spread your group out. That can use up time in reassembling for group activities. But with forethought, it certainly can be worked out. For home stays, I recommend housing at least two or more of your group per house. To me, it is just more comforting to know that there are at least a couple of our group together should trouble occur. Be sure to ask what bedding, meals and transportation are included by the host family. And inquire about what may be appropriate presents that your members might give to their host family.

Dorm–Style Lodging

It is common for groups of young people to be housed in dormitory–style housing. Sometimes this may be in a school from which classroom furniture is removed, bedding brought in, and visiting groups are assigned. This can be a team–building situation and provides the opportunity for the group to stay more compact. Whether in a school classroom or actual dormitory, make sure that you get specifics on access to restrooms, showers, laundry, and meal service. Unless your ground schedule matches the access times to these facilities, you may find yourself in a mess. I had one team in a dorm where the shower was only available from 7:00 to 8:00 AM. That did not work well as we were a soccer team with games throughout the day and no place to clean up afterwards. Make your list of these items to ask your tour agent or site contact ahead of time.

Hotels: Hamburger or Filet Mignon?

Youth groups and hotels can work well if you match them carefully. When we travel, most of us enjoy the amenities that the finer hotels may offer, but like the old "bull in a china shop" scenario, there can be trouble in paradise. As mentioned earlier, the high energy and activity level of most youth needs an outlet. Refined hotels filled with antiques and delicate art may not be the best match for those members, and therefore your whole group.

Whether you or the tour operators are arranging the hotel, it's usually the same criteria: location, size and price. Once you find the right match, other factors like swimming pools, spas, access to parks and beaches, buffet meals, proximity to local sites of interest, and presence of other youth groups in the same facility are just frosting on the cake. When we have traveled in both the US and in Europe, we have made it known that we like smaller, family-run hotels. They usually reflect the personality of the region that you are visiting, and a better cultural experience than larger, chain hotels can offer. They are often more low-key and absorb a youth group with less effort. We have also found the food to be more reflective of the local culture. The hotel stay with players and boosters together also keeps your whole group more intact, and this can simplify organizing trips and transfers.

Salvatore, second from left, presents our group with a Team Seattle cake. He and his family own and operate a small hotel in Cesenatico, Italy and made us feel like we were his special relatives. Joining Salvatore and Larry are coaches Tim Self (l) and Doug Terrel (r).

Transportation Issues
Ground Transportation
These boots were made for walkin'

While on your trip, you want to plan as little time "in transit" as possible. Not only are transfers from point A to point B tedious in the loading and unloading portions, but also they take away from your time to do fun and interesting things. Of course there are sightseeing excursions that provide a nice addition to any trip, but with young people, these usually mean "nap time." Choose carefully.

Every time you need to load and unload, there is potential for stress from delays to tardy members. Keep your itinerary simple with as few ground transfers as is possible.

Event Transportation

At some destinations, your host organization may provide shuttles. These shuttles usually serve many participants and operate on schedules that are convenient for the overall program schedule. But these schedules may require that your group leave several hours earlier than your game/performance would need. Also you may have a considerable wait afterwards. Ask in advance how this works.

Many groups, including some of our own teams, have experienced great difficulties with event transportation. Some groups have actually been late or missed entirely their game/performance. The bottom line is to inquire **in advance** with people who plan these shuttle schedules, and with people who have used them at this site in past years. Their tips will be invaluable.

Afoot in the Village

For reasonable distances, walking is our recommendation for getting around. It uses up some of that energy that the youth seem to always have, and is good for the rest of us. Your itinerary can be planned in advance to create the "on foot" opportunities for your members. By doing this, they will see things that they would have missed at 35 mile per hour. Granted, you cannot cover as much area as you could by "wheeled" transportation, but you cannot see everything anyway. Keep it simple. Most of the favorite memories of our members were from experiences on such on–foot explorations. When such a transfer is necessary, consider the most cost–effective and stress–free option.

Charter Buses

Private buses show up at your lodging and whisk you away to your destination. They are usually reserved for your members only and you don't have to worry about seating space or pickpockets. Your driver is also just that: **your** driver. They are there to serve just your group.

A comfortable bus with a restroom and a video screen will make your travel much more relaxing, and allow for longer distances between breaks if you have a long way to go.

Public Buses

Public bus transportation can be another alternative, but remember that the schedules are inflexible, the space is usually open to all users, not just your group, and they go on specific routes. To get to a site, you may need to transfer one or more times over, then back. Will this be workable with your group?

Mass Transit

The pros and cons of mass transit (subways, bullet trains, elevated trams) are similar to those of public buses. They are usually fast, reasonably priced and go to the center of most cities. From there you need other transportation or need to walk. It is common for security to be a consideration with mass transit as pickpockets thrive there. Just be smart and stay in groups.

Group members traveling in a rental van.

Rental Cars/Vans

Rental cars offer the epitome of flexibility. They are there at your beck and call. But you must plan for parking, caravanning to events and fuel stops. For open days, they give the group the maximum access to the area, but are expensive and have limited capacity. While in Austria at a tournament, we rented a 9–passenger van to shuttle us around the village of Wolfsberg. It was a great help with our 4 teams, and my family used it for our personal travel the following week, after the team had returned home.

Whatever your reason for traveling with your group (tournament, musical performance, other competition), you need to make the most of your other time. Making this part of your pre–trip planning will enrich the adventure even more. As you will probably not have time to do and to see everything that you would like at your destination, prioritizing will help you key in on a few selections. Once you have those identified, you can begin making inquiries for the "how–tos," or you can again use your tour operator. They will have an established network to connect your group into those selections. They also can counsel you if you have missed a major site or event at your destination. A good agent will also help you plan what days and times to see busy sites, to buy advance tickets where possible, and to take advantage of group access gates. The agent can recommend guides where applicable, and to get the best fees. Keep in mind; some agents will have an additional fee for these planning services. Make sure you keep asking if there are such additional charges.

We Want to Do It All

We also suggest that you do not book your group too tightly. Work around one or two planned events per day. That allows you flexibility should you need to change you schedule. Remember to allow for free days to let members "do their own thing."

> With a tip from our agent, we called a coach who a year earlier had visited the Alpencup in Wolfsburg, Austria. He told us about Wolfsburg Castle, where, with advance arrangements, a group could have lunch. We set that up and were the only team that had access to the castle that year.

One call started the arrangements that led to a great experience by having lunch in a real castle. The kids were really impressed.

On our 1999 trip, we stayed in Verona for the Italy Cup. Not just famous for being the home of Romeo and Juliet, Verona boasts the third largest Roman arena ever built. Made over 2,000 years ago, it is the most intact remaining Roman arena and is still used all summer for opera and concerts. With a tip from our agent, we were able to book group tickets in advance, and attend an incredible performance of the opera *Tosca*. About 50 of the players attended, and most agreed with our son Adam, who summed up the experience as "the most incredible place and the most boring entertainment." But we all were glad we got the word from the agent.

The 2,000 year-old Verona arena.

Chapter 4

Enrollment Procedure

Keeping Track of Member Details

The Deposit

After families have been through your orientation process and have decided to join your group, you need to make them "put their money where their mouth is" by getting a per–person deposit. We have charged $200.00 per–person in the past. People will put more thought into a serious commitment before they have to write a big check. These are the serious individuals and families that you want. You don't want people to book and later cancel, although this happens because emergencies will occasionally arise.

Once you have that deposit, we suggest that you start a family account page or file (see Appendix A). We use a simple Excel file to list the information. We track check number, date, and amount of each deposit and payment. Just before the final payment is due, we have usually mailed a copy of this statement to each family.

Enrollment Forms

Receipt of this deposit will generate a mailing to all of the new member/s that includes:

A Cover Letter (see Appendix B for sample) with specifics about the amount of deposit received, a payment schedule, a request for self–addressed, stamped, legal–sized envelopes for return mailings, a brief explanation of the forms listed below, and a request for two copies of their photo ID (student body card, driver's license, or passport if leaving the country)

*The Member Information Sheet (see Appendix B1)

A Liability Release Form **for minors** under 18 (see Appendix B2–a)

A Liability Release Form **for travelers** (see Appendix B2–b)

*A Guardianship Form for those under 18 NOT traveling with a parent (see Appendix B3)

*A Medical Release Form for those under 18 (see Appendix B4)

*An <u>Alcohol Release Form</u> for those under 21 NOT traveling with a parent (see Appendix B5)

A <u>Traveler's Agreement of Behavior Information Sheet</u> (see Appendix B6–a)

An <u>Agreement of Behavior For</u> Travelers (see Appendix B6–b)

Note that some of these forms require a notary stamp and signature.

* Note: The above four asterisks indicate the forms you should take with you on your trip.

As you can see, some forms apply only to youth travelers **NOT** traveling with a parent. If Mom and/or Dad are along on the trip, they are in charge of their own children. If not, the guardian and group leader need legal documents to use in cases of legal or medical emergencies. We also put into the cover letter a request that these documents and forms be sent back to us as soon as possible.

Once the forms are returned, you need to develop a system for filing them. We actually buy a portable filing box made of heavy duty plastic for storage before and after the trip. Some of these forms will be taken on the trip with you, so a smaller file folder will also be needed.

Official Documentation

Depending on what type of group, your destination (foreign or domestic) and the age of your members, you may need to do some research on what the necessary paperwork is. Lack of required documentation and approved forms may stop your group in its tracks. It can also cause legal problems for some or for the entire group.

Some organizations have regional, national and international criteria that must be met before you can leave your hometown. Your State Association, for example, may need you to complete forms and rosters, and submit them for scrutiny. Customs and immigration will always have criteria. There may be fees for this as well. Don't take "hearsay" as the law with these requirements. Make contact with that office and be specific about your program and itinerary so that their answers can meet your needs.

> I was with one group in England where they found that one of their youth members would not be permitted back into the US after the trip. Although this player had lived most of his life in the US, he only had a Mexican passport. When the group left, the airline begrudgingly let him on the plane to England. Coming home was a different matter. Without a travel visa (issued by the US Embassy), a foreign passport holder cannot come into the country. The London office of the US Embassy had no appointments for six weeks, so the group leaders had to fly the player directly to Mexico City via Amsterdam and at a cost of $5,400 plus the expense of the unaccompanied minor escort with each airline and each airport. It was a very stressful end to a great trip

Coach's Documentation

In addition to the appropriate forms in the section above, we also have the coach sign a "Coach's Agreement" (Appendix F). This clarifies our expectations on such things as timely response to emails and calls, participation in specific planning meetings, and a behavior code that is over and above that of the "Traveler's Agreement of Behavior Information Sheet" (Appendix B6-a). Your coach, bandleader or teacher represents the entire group and is a key figure. This is why we go to the trouble to discuss this with them, and have them sign the agreement.

You may not feel the need to use such a form, but it has been invaluable to us when a situation arises where the coach is not stepping up to the plate as promised.

Allow time to process required documents like
passports, visas or parental consent forms.

There also may be special requirements at your destinations. Some of your host organizations or municipalities may also have such forms and need particular information about your group and its members. It might also help to contact a group leader who has done this type of travel recently. Their lessons learned may save you some grief. With any of these required documents, begin the process as soon as possible. Some approval may take months and some offices charge late fees if you submit too close to your departure date.

For foreign travel, passports are another critical detail that your members may need to obtain. Find out what local offices are available, and share that information. Also inform your members what is needed at their visit (2 passport photos, birth certificate, cash versus checks, hours of operation). In today's travel climate since 9-11, it is a good idea to have your passport processed 6 months before the beginning of the tour.

Bookkeeping Details

Payment Schedule

As mentioned above, a payment schedule is outlined in the cover letter. To get the per–payment amount, we simply divide the trip cost less deposit by the number of months until we leave. We require their final payment 30 days prior to leaving. We also have skipped December and January (holiday bills) and April (tax time) in those calculations. That increases the monthly amount due on the other months, but we've found the members appreciate avoiding payments during those financial crunch times.

We have set a rule that the payments are due in our mailbox by the first of the month. You can set whatever schedule works for your group. Be strict and we suggest having late fees. You are doing so much to make this trip happen, the members should be able to get their payments to you on time. You will be making payments to various uniform and tour companies, and they expect their money on time. We also use emails as gentle reminders if we have a late payment, and we have used other group leaders/coaches to call families who are not paying per the agreement. In some cases, an alternative payment plan will work better for some families. Make them put it into writing and send it to you. The final payment must still be in before you depart. Most tour companies will want their final installments 30 days in advance.

Individual Deviations

Some members may prefer to spend extra time at their destinations. They may wish to leave a few days before the group does, or stay on a few days afterwards. Check with your tour company and airline to see if they will allow this. If so, there is usually a "Deviation Charge." That charge should be passed on to those individuals. Appendix C shows the <u>Traveler Trip Detail Confirmation</u> form that we have used to confirm travelers' flight plans as we understand them. The purpose of this form is to make any travel plan misunderstandings surface well in advance of the trip. There is space for deviation description and charges. There is also a place at the bottom for their signature. After signing, they need to keep a photocopy for themselves, and return the signed and dated original to you. File these for safekeeping.

Sharing Information

To share information, we usually email and mail updates to all families. Using a "Group List" on your email server is quick and gets through to multiple email addresses with the same family. You may select US mail using the envelopes requested of each family in the cover letter. (see Appendix B for sample). We have key group leaders rotate in helping to stuff the mailed updates.

Web–friendly updates can be via email or on your website, if you have one. A trip webpage is a wonderful tool. It can be used to post these updates, trip destination pictures and facts, travel dates and contact information. It can market your project to a wide audience and can collect historical data if you are doing more than one of these trips. In almost every group, there is talent ready and waiting to help you develop such a site. And the cost can be minimal with tips like posting advertisements of sponsors, schools or clubs. You can also use their sites to link to yours and the reverse.

We also have produced three or four newsletters prior to the trip. The members have appreciated them as they are more detailed than some of the emails. Information on your itinerary and internet links to some of them, deadlines for items like passports or travel insurance, and hints on what to expect at your destination have all been well received. Members have also commented that this printed newsletter is something that they continued to use as a reference before and after the trip.

Data Maintenance

As mentioned earlier, deposits and payments from members must be tracked and recorded. Payments to vendors also must be recorded. Computer files are very helpful and easy to use.

A roster for each group is necessary. You will need a roster for the youth team or band, one for the whole group including boosters, one for flight groups, hotel groups and bus groups. These rosters will help key group leaders be aware of who is in their respective groups.

Files must be set up and maintained to handle these forms. You will also need to decide who has access to your trip files. Some of the information may be sensitive and should not be shared (birthdates of parents from their ID for example). Be conscious about this and proceed with care.

We also recommend being diligent about keeping these records and files current. The closer you come to your departure date, the more details that will surface and need your attention. If you keep your paperwork current, you will be thankful in the end.

Chapter 5

Fundraising

The Buck Starts Here

Who Needs Help

As most groups are a mix of families from many walks of life and of varying incomes, the per-person cost of your trip will be more feasible for some than for others. How you accommodate those individuals or families who need financial help is up to your group. If you do wish to offer assistance, you must make the process known, listing what information the family needing assistance must give you, like what you wish to know about their need, who that information is sent to, by what deadline, and define who in your group will make the final decision. We also suggest that you make all information received confidential and keep your decisions limited within a small committee.

When Enough is Enough

Most youth teams, clubs and schools are eternally involved in raising money for various causes. This makes adding another fundraiser to their respective plates a little difficult. In our family's case, I knew that I'd saturated our market when my own mother politely passed on buying the "item of the week." In this case, it was wrapping paper that we were selling to raise money for the boys' baseball team. You may experience similar results, complete with a slight headache!

Also, the time that is needed to do any fundraiser cuts into our already hectic schedules. We have had some parents tell us that they'd rather just write a check rather than have to coerce their child into a marketing mode. Alternately, some young people really love to sell stuff at the supermarket, or door-to-door in their neighborhood. But all that aside, for group fundraising, you must decide how much each family will benefit financially from their respective involvement. You need to figure this out before you proceed.

A fundraiser where all are expected to contribute a set amount may be one answer. If doing an auction or selling something (pepperoni, wrapping paper, magazines, candy), you can set a specific dollar amount that is required of each family. That gives them the choice of just writing a check (if they have deep pockets), or get out there and solicit donations or sell items. Everyone's contribution into the pot is equal.

Now what happens to the funds in the pot? Do you apply those monies equally to each family, or do you have special needs for scholarships where they are channeled to particular individuals who have been identified as deserving help? If the latter is the case, you must be up-front with the group **before** the fundraiser commences so that there are no bad feelings.

Who is In, Who Is Not?

During our boys' school years, we have done almost every kind of fundraiser that you can imagine. For these youth travel groups, we find that it is better to plan fundraisers that are voluntary. This allows each family to decide at what level they wish to participate. Then if they do, all the rewards go into their account and are not shared. Car washes were a disaster as everyone worked all day, and once the money was divided between all the families, each only got about $20.00. Now this is different if a group is raising money to buy something for that group, like new sports or band equipment, a donation to a member's family having a medical emergency, or a memorial plaque for a school or club.

Good examples of fundraisers that rewarded families based on effort given included poinsettia sales and raffles for big prizes like a car or trip. Our tour company even got involved and donated the trip and provided the raffle tickets at no cost to our groups. Ask the companies that you interview if they have such programs.

Options

Another thing to investigate is whether or not your group qualifies for the IRS non–profit, 501 C–3 status. If so, this opens new horizons for you and makes donors eligible for tax credits. This will make your fundraiser more attractive when marketing it. Depending on your state tax structure, having such a status may save you sales tax when you purchase items to sell. That is money back in your families' pockets.

Matching funds from parents' employers is another fundraising method worth bringing up to all members. For every dollar donated by the employee, these employers may also give an additional percentage to your fund or even match it dollar–for–dollar up to certain limits. Companies like Microsoft are known for such generous programs.

Advertising your fundraiser within your community may also generate more funds and alert them that should people approach them for a sale or donation, it is a legitimate cause. We have used the school newsletters, our local community newspapers and sometimes limited mailings. Provide a contact person, phone and email/website should they wish connect with your members.

Guarding the Treasure Chest

Once you are accumulating monies from your fundraisers, keep careful records of all contributions. Keep separate family accounts if needed. Each family will be very protective of the money that they personally raised. You will need to have impeccable records to adequately keep them informed and to answer their questions. We have kept track of dates, amounts and check numbers where applicable. People can get very touchy over money matters, and justly so, as they were the ones who worked for this money.

Chapter 6

Gifts

Paving the Way for Special Treatment

Why? Because of our wonderful parents, we were both raised to bring a small gift to a host or hostess when invited to their home. This concept, when applied to our travels, has really opened doors for us and rewarded us with the royal treatment from hosts around the world.

When you travel with a group, you are going to encounter a wide variety of people who are working (sometimes for pay and sometimes not) to make your visit pleasant and organized. Such people may include event organizers (sports tournaments, musical and talent performances), guides, drivers, hotel management, coaches, band leaders, and club and city officials (presidents, mayors, ambassadors). It is amazing how even a small token gift when given to such people will be paid back tenfold in other services and kindnesses. Bringing gifts is not expected—the intent is just to thank these people for what they have already done. But we have been well rewarded in return.

During our first day at a small family-run hotel in Chioggia, Italy, the owners were courteous, but certainly did not make any extra efforts on our group's behalf. At the second dinner, we presented the wife with a package of foods from our city, a polo to her husband and hand-crocheted trivets to his elderly mother. They proudly showed all the neighbors these gifts and from that moment treated us as very special guests. Their English even improved and they were more patient with our Italian.

Another very large hotel near Verona was consistently blaming our players for any problems that surfaced. As there were dozens of other European teams also lodging there, we seemed to be the easy scapegoat. Once we presented the manager with one of our gift packages, things changed markedly. The staff showed much more tolerance for our own infractions of the rules, and the German team became the new scapegoat.

Collecting the Goodies
What's Nice and What's Not

To come up with a pile of loot to distribute, network your members. It is ideal to get all the items donated versus spending "group funds." And remember, because you are traveling, the items that you receive are the items you must pack and carry along with you. We are very specific with what types of items we like to collect for trip gifts.

We prefer gifts that:

- Are lightweight and are not easily broken, torn or crushed

- Are **NOT** highly flammable or explosive

- Reflect your area. For our Seattle food products we have taken Starbuck's coffee grounds, Oberto sausage products, shelf–stable packages of smoked salmon, Applets and Cotlets, Boehm's chocolates and one or two bottles of local wine.

- Showcase your local sports teams, radio stations, and sightseeing highlights. Again, for us Sonics tee shirts, Mariners caps, stickers and key chains from radio stations, and Space Needle souvenirs.

- Reflect your group's logo. If you order uniforms, it may be possible to add a few extra tee shirts with the logo and use them as gifts. Hats and polos are also popular.

Organizing Your Search For Donations

When networking with your group for sources, assign businesses to specific people so that your potential donors won't get hit several times by several of your members. Families who offer to do this may purchase some of these items themselves. Others may be donated by the companies and organizations. Be sure to let them know if you are a non–profit organization, as it will make it easier for the company to donate. This falls under the same IRS non-profit 501-C-3 deduction regulation discussed in the last chapter.

Don't be shy about taking items that are dated. Shirts, hats, pins and patches from last year's tournament, promotion, or team/company logo have little value to the donors, but your hosts will not care if the shirt has last year's design or year on it. They will be thrilled with the gift anyway.

Specific Gift Ideas

For tournament gifts team–to–team, a club pennant is traditional. If you do not have one, you can usually buy them from your state association (soccer, baseball, football). It can be expensive to have them custom–made, but check into local shops that do embroidery work as well as with the larger national companies. See what you can afford for the quantity needed. Like the shirts and logos mentioned earlier, you might be able to purchase last year's pennants for a better price, provided they are not marked with an old date.

For higher profile gifts such as to a mayor or tournament director, we will package several items together with clear cellophane wrap and ribbon that we bring along bulk for assembly on–site. We top such packages with small US and Washington State flags. These create a great impression and will make your group look very appreciative and professional.

Tee shirts and caps make great gifts for drivers, coaches and team captains. For more personal gifts for your guides, home–stay families and event hosts, we also make gift packages. Oftentimes, these will include personal items like lotions, inexpensive jewelry, books about our area and even handcrafted gifts. American movie posters (available at most video rental stores) are also very popular, inexpensive gifts if traveling outside the US.

Wagons Ho!
Ideas For Inventorying and Packing

Now that you have all this stuff, what do you do with it? We inventory **everything** and have a general plan for who we expect to present gifts to. We also plan on having several items available for impromptu gifts. Keep a couple gifts in your carry-on bag.

Packing your inventory is important as you must find containers and luggage that will travel well. We have used heavy-duty Rubbermaid-like totes with wheels. Old, hard-sided luggage can also work. Depending on your mode of transportation, the containers may take a lot of abuse. For this reason, items that break or crush easily are not the best to solicit.

We have used uniforms and tee shirts to pack around the other boxes, cans and packages. They buffer things well and are light.

If I do take a local wine or beer for a gift, I wrap the bottle in bubble wrap, fold cardboard around that, and use duct tape to secure the top, bottom and sides. I pack that with shirts that could be washed should the bottle break. I have never lost a bottle yet.

Speaking of "poundage," check with your transportation agent and make sure to know the restrictions on the weight and size limit of your luggage. If you mess up on this one, you'll be repacking at the airport or train depot. That is not a pretty sight. And ask what security access you will run into. They may need access into your containers and luggage. If so, taping the totes shut should be done after the security check is complete.

> Flying into Barcelona with 84 people, a mountain of luggage, and not knowing the distance to our busses, I recruited two young men and their freight carts to assist us. Pulling two Nike shirts from my bag was all the persuasion they needed. With my bribery, they became "ours." These carts, by the way, were the same large carts that sky captains use.

Chapter 7

Trip Uniforms

Ideas on Specialty Uniforms for Your Trip

For many existing sports and performance teams, providing uniforms may be a non–issue for your trip. Such groups will have the attire that they use for their local season. But for travel groups organized for specialty trips, members may be in need of jerseys, blazers, warm–ups, windbreakers, sox, shorts, and even shoes. These can be very costly. The selection, sizing, ordering and distributing processes will all take a great deal of time. The following are a few important things that we have learned over the years.

What You Need As A Minimum

We suggest that you simplify the items needed as much as is possible. If this uniform is only to be used for this trip, don't complicate your life as the organizer by trying to get too fancy or elaborate. Assign a uniform planning committee but keep it small. The more people that are involved, the longer the process will take.

Determine what, at minimum, you absolutely need. That's where you start. Now price those basics and see how it affects your budget. You can always expand your matching travel wardrobe if money and your time allow it.

And when planning what you need, build in what you think most members may already have: black dress shoes; a white, long sleeved shirt; soccer cleats; white sports socks, etc. This saves you planning time and can help keep your costs down.

Sizing

When you have decided what apparel the group needs, and have selected a vendor, get examples of each garment in all sizes (small, medium, large, extra large) and have members try them on. Have these garments accessible in a convenient location under the watch of a responsible person who will tally the requests.

Alternatives to Buying Uniforms

There are several ways that you can obtain the travel wardrobe without paying full price. One solution is to borrow the necessary items from local groups that you can contact. We have borrowed player uniforms, for example. Perhaps you could borrow sports jackets from the band, choir or debate club at your local school. Network with your members for resources. If you are a non-profit organization, the group that you borrow from may be able to write off a "rental" fee. Or you may be able to pay a small rental fee that is considerably less that the cost of purchase. It still saves you money. The downfall of borrowing or renting uniforms of any type is that you must pay for lost or damaged pieces. This will invariably happen with youth travel groups.

Buying the needed attire and including it in the cost of the trip has its benefits. As everyone literally owns their uniform, they are responsible for it and must replace it if damaged or lost, and can do with it as they choose after the trip is over. In the case of travel jerseys, at the end of the trip the players will often trade with players from other cities or countries. Other members like to keep them as a personal souvenir. In either case, it gives the members options.

Quality, and therefore cost, will vary widely with apparel and shoes. If your members will only wear these items ten to twenty times, it may not make sense to spend a lot of money. We have spent as little as $10 for a jersey that looked good and served our needs. Conversely, we have spent more on apparel with no different impact. I would prefer that we put our dollars into other perks for the trip. Having a famous brand uniform makes us feel good, but might make your budget tight in other categories.

Some groups already have uniforms which eliminates a lot of work But you still might choose to have trip tee shirts or polos with a trip logo.

Group polos and t-shirts come in a wide variety of styles, sizes
and colors and make great souvenirs and gifts.

Trip Apparel Options

We have also offered optional "trip" sweatshirts, polos, hats and tee shirts to the members for an additional cost. These are very popular and make packing simpler. The trip logo can be added to these and makes another good souvenir before and after the trip. While in your community, it does not hurt to have members wearing advertising about your group. It may help with recruiting and fundraising as well. You can order extras of a few of these items to be used as team gifts.

Some individuals need specialty items. A soccer goalie or baseball catcher will need additional gear for that position. Or a drum major will need a different uniform. You will have to decide which items you will provide and pay for, and which you expect them to supply. Discuss this with such members when they sign on. You don't want to have to deal with stressful last–minute surprises.

For numbered apparel, remember that people all have favorite, or lucky numbers. It may be *nice* to ask them for their top three choices if you have the extra time, but be prepared for extra work in the ordering process. The easiest way is to order the apparel in the necessary size and just give it to the individuals with an assigned, random number.

Another tip is ordering a simple tee shirt as a part of the member's wardrobe. It can be used as a "travel uniform" to keep track of members at airports and train stations, and can be numbered if desired and used as the alternate jersey if there is a conflict in colors with another team. Each member has always received a free tee shirt from our tour operator, and we have used them for these purposes.

And above all, stress to your group about ordering and bringing clothing that can be hand washed and line dried. Not all sites on your trip will have laundry facilities.

Chapter 8

Roles, Responsibilities and Division of Labor
Dictatorship Or Democracy?

We truly believe that the dozens and even hundreds of hours of work that we have spent planning and implementing our adventures have been time well spent. It is an enormous commitment, but well worth it. The memories are all priceless treasures and an opportunity for you and your child that should not be missed. With that said, there is still a great deal of work to be done. Here are some areas that we would recommend adding to your planning process. Remember that we are speaking in the context of before, during and after the trip itself.

Leadership Structure

Depending on what type of youth group you are (athletic team like soccer, baseball or basketball; musical group like a band or choir; or talent team like cheer, debate or gymnastics), you may inherit some hierarchy. Bandleaders, coaches, managers or trainers may immediately be involved by association. But with the hundreds of details that need attention, these individuals may or may not wish to play a key role in the trip's planning phase.

It seems that most groups find a parent or two who step forward and become the tour coordinators or "tour leaders." The individuals mentioned above will want to be involved, but to what extent must be determined. If you are one of those who have stepped forward to work on the planning committee, be specific during your initial conversations. Once you decide what needs to be done, make sure that you are clear who is responsible, and set goals that detail the deadlines. As things progress, reevaluate the workload, and add new assignments to those who can follow through with them in a timely manner. The further along into the planning phase you are, the more things that will surface and require attention. Although we prefer a small planning committee, don't hesitate to add more members if needed. Don't max–out yourself or other members. Be realistic with assignments. Tap into members' strengths (computer skills, fundraising, research work).

Group, or Tour Leaders

If you were hiring this as a position, the ad could read:

Group Tour Leader
Responsible, high–energy
person needed to
coordinate all phases of
planning, organizing,
implementing and
monitoring the details
needed to result in a
successful trip for our
youth group. Strong
inter–personal skills,
efficient, organizational
mind, and good
multi–tasking ability are
necessary. Must be flexible,
patient and able to
delegate. No salary or
healthcare benefits
available, but great
personal satisfaction may
result. Send résumé to P.O.
Box 4484

The group leaders need to be self–motivated and able to see the whole picture. They must be able to keep their focus amidst constant interruptions and to filter the many needs of the group. We have always paired up as group leaders, and divided the oversight of different areas between us.

Group leaders must also follow the project through to its fruition. There is the pre–trip phase, the trip itself, and the post trip wrap up. Keeping on course through all of these is the key to a successful trip.

The Group must also agree to work under the leadership of the appointed group leaders. Keeping the members aware of "the plan," "the process" and the people that are making them function is important. Everyone should feel comfortable in speaking their minds, but it is the key organizers who must make the judgment calls.

If you are the group leader, keep reminding yourself of how this project fits in with the overall scheme of the world and your life. Try not to become the "tour dictator." It is probably not the most successful method for getting the job done. And don't make this project consume your life. Keep a balance, release some of the duties, and look to the young people for motivation. They are the ones that you are doing this for. Not the other adults, but the band, team or club members.

> The grandmother of one of our players had hesitated about attending orientation meeting about that trip. After multiple emails and phone messages, I finally reached her.
>
> Her concern about going on this trip was from a past experience. She and her husband had been on a guided tour where the leader refused to deviate from the itinerary. He kept such a packed and tight schedule, that his group secretly labeled him the "travel Nazi." If anyone in that group was off schedule by even a couple minutes, the leader came unglued and punished the whole group as if they were children.
>
> As a group leader, set realistic schedules, but build in flexibility. The members appreciate it and when special situations arise that you'd like to include, you can allow them. Don't carry a stopwatch and treat the travelers like an efficiency expert. Remember, this is supposed to be fun.

Establish your means of communication with the other committee members and group members, and set expectations on acceptable response times. We have always asked that we get an answer back within 24 hours unless otherwise specified. We also get email addresses, and both cell and home phone numbers for everyone to allow easier access. To keep the planning process going, you need information in a timely manner.

While on the trip, determine who is the point person in contacting people and agencies as you arrive in places:

- Who lets the airline check–in staff or train station representative know that your group has arrived?

- Who seeks out the ground transportation desk?

- Who is first into the lodging site?

- Who initially meets the event officials?

- Who initiates interaction between your group and others?

- Who speaks on behalf of your group at formal and informal gatherings?

- Who deals with emergencies that require hospital care or that involve local law enforcement who has issues with any of your members?

There is not just one answer to these, nor one person who will always be available. If you've discussed these situations, you can have Plan A, and Plan B. These may or may not be in writing, but your key members will know what to do, rather than keeping the group in limbo while you work through this at a site.

After the trip is over, we suggest that you consider some of the ideas listed in the "Post–Trip" chapter. They add to the overall experience, but still require planning and coordination. The group leader will still be involved in this final chapter of your trip.

Committee Members

The other planning committee members will most likely come from within your ranks as you notify the group what help is needed (subliminal message: Keep the committee small). Your coach or bandleader may have recommendations of whom you might contact. When you make contact, be clear and concise about what you need, what the process will be, and what the boundaries of each position are. This will allow your potential co–planners to better decide if they are able to commit to helping. Consider personality styles that are compatible to yours. It is vital that you, as group leader, and the committee members, get to know each other very well. It is equally necessary that you, as the group leader, be in charge and a clear manager who, at the same time, is not overbearing. Being up–front and realistic makes everybody's jobs easier and avoids future problems.

Coaches, Bandleaders, and Trainers

Your youth members share a common talent, ability and knowledge. That is the reason you are planning this adventure. They could be musicians, athletes or debaters. They wish to share, demonstrate or test themselves in different locations. Many people have probably helped to plant, promote and polish these qualities. Your current coach, trainer or bandleader is the "shepherd of this flock" and has great value in that capacity. As mentioned earlier, these people may or may not want to play a key role in the production of your trip.

Working with cooperative coaches who can share in our travel
plan has made our trips a pleasure. Here, we celebrate our arrival
at the Holland Cup. Larry, Coach Rich Borton, Mary Kay, Kathy
Robison and Coach Mark Robison share the Dutch hospitality.

As we believe that these individuals do enough by working with the youth, we try to let them do just that. We agree on the goals of the trip and include them in all updates. Other than that, we have other people take the roles in the trip planning and implementation processes. We do have a "Coach's Agreement" (Appendix F) that clarifies our expectations of them in advance. We give them 2 copies, one of which we want back dated and signed.

At the destinations, we build in time for the youth members to practice per their coach. We provide the venue for those practices with coach input. We suggest that you consider doing likewise. It gives that coach autonomy during practices, performances, games or competitions. Other than those times, the group is under the direction of other adults (guardians, group leaders, guides, hosts).

Parents

Before the Trip

For the pre-planning phase of your trip, you can tap into the talents of your youth members' parents. Use them to investigate uniform sources, destination and travel information, fundraising potential, and trip promotion sites. Be specific with them as to what you need and how you plan on using the information provided. Have them bring their findings back to your committee, and then proceed with your planning and decisions. Listen to their ideas and suggestions, but stay in control. Be flexible enough to change your plan if they do come up with a valuable and usable idea. Make them feel appreciated for the time and effort put forth.

During the Trip

For those parents who are going on the trip as boosters and guardians, find helpful ways to involve them that are a benefit to your youth group. They usually enjoy participating and can take some burden off of other group leaders.

We have used boosters as bus captains who can assist in roll call as you board the bus or train, to organize the loading and unloading of the mountain of luggage, to help with on–board meal or snack service, and to disseminate information.

If traveling out of the US, having any members who may speak the local language is a huge plus. Knowing a little Japanese, French or Spanish will make traveling so much easier.

One great benefit for touring foreign countries is the ability to look and shop at wonderful places like this produce market in Cannes, France.

Boosters have also been assigned to take smaller groups on more personal tours of museums and other tourist and historical sights. If a booster knows this in advance, he or she can do a little research and add a positive angle to that outing. This small group concept works well in busy areas or in large cities where you want to keep close track of the youth members.

If staying in one place for a few days where the group will have free time to explore, you can assign the job of "team scout" to one or more boosters. They check out interesting sights, hours of operation and the local transportation schedules and costs. Scoping out the local banks and currency exchange booths is also helpful.

Regardless of where you travel in the US or around the world, most of us want to bring home a few souvenirs. Many boosters are great shoppers and are excellent resources to find out the local specialties or crafts, and where to find the best deals. Most towns have market days where temporary stalls are set up that sell everything from shoes to shish kabobs. These markets are fun and provide an excellent alternative to the malls.

It is a nice touch to have a couple of trip photographers and someone with a video camera. For formal group photos at key sites, or for those casual moments, they will be ready to go with few arrangements. These pictures and videos can capture moments for the group that will make great post-trip souvenirs.

Boosters can orchestrate the gift exchanges between your group and others. This entails getting the members organized, usually in a line, with the appropriate gift item in their hand; then, on cue, to proceed one–by–one in the exchange.

Most importantly, these boosters must be responsible for following the rules and schedule of the trip. If the youth group members see that the adults show up late or don't follow the rules, then they will not be as motivated to do so.

Host clubs will oftentimes hold an informal reception for your group. Assign someone to find out what the general format will be so your group can be prepared with gifts and thank-you speeches. Here, coaches Bob Rupp, Jessica Netherlands and Terry Conway join Larry at Club Nice.

Guardians

We have always been strict that all youth travelers under 18 have an assigned and documented guardian. For those youth members traveling with at least one parent, that parent is automatically their legal guardian. For those youths traveling without a parent, it is necessary to match them up with an adult who becomes their guardian. For some small groups, your coach, band leader or trainer will assume that responsibility. As we have always offered the trip to parents as well, we have tried to maximize on those adults as guardians. We feel that the coaches do enough already. Your group will need to analyze this issue depending on your format and number of adults joining you.

We have always made the guardians responsible for their charges while on tours. Here the players and boosters tour a perfumery in the village of Eze on the French Riviera. The guardians are expected to know the whereabouts of their 'trip kids' at all times.

Our Golden Rule

The coach is responsible for the players from the time that we gather for games, practices or performances, during the transit to and from sites, and during the event. The guardian is responsible for them at all other times.

In Appendix B3 you will see a sample of the guardianship form that we have used. It requires a notary's signature and stamp.

We provide guardians a list of expectations to help them with their "trip family." These include:

- Representing their youth traveler in matters of medical need, legal entanglements and group rule infringements

- Securing documents like passports and player cards

- Keeping the "extra" cash and all the credit and debit cards

- Doing an initial damage inspection upon move–in to a lodging site, and doing the final damage inspection upon move–out

- Testing the TV remote if applicable (broken/lost ones cost $$$)

- Setting expectations of free–time activities (where, with whom, how long)

- Establishing the player check–in and check–out routine for free–time excursions that do not include the guardian

- Performing bed checks at curfew when applicable

- Keeping on schedule with the itinerary (meals, packing, loading)

- Having players send postcards and buy gifts for appropriate people (like Mom and Dad if not along, grandparents or sponsors/benefactors)

It is up to the guardian to enforce the group's rules. We have some rules that can mean immediate return home at their family's expense. All travelers with our groups sign an agreement listing such rules. See Traveler's Agreement Form Appendix B6–a. As yet, we have not had to enforce any punitive action, but it is necessary to set up your rules in advance and make it clear what the repercussions will be for those who do not follow them.

Youth Members

Players, band members or teammates are expected to step up to the plate and be responsible for themselves. Once we have made it clear what we expect, we have found that these members are the best. They are flexible, reasonable and provide the adult members with a motivating and unending supply of enthusiasm. They truly keep you young.

Making the youth members aware of the rules and allowing them input has proven to us that they will act responsibly.

Our Other Golden Rule

Keep restrictions limited until the youth members have demonstrated that they need them.

We suggest that you be clear and concise with your expectations. Give updates as you proceed with the planning, and during the trip. Include them in the planning when possible, and ask them what they need to meet your expectations. A good example would be telling them to be up early for an event or departure. They may not know how to arrange a wake up call, or may not have a clock or watch with an alarm. Providing them with a wake–up mechanism helps them succeed and meet your expectations.

Below are listed some of our expectations from past trips:

- Show respect to others and respect local customs and cultures.

- Pack and transport your own luggage.

- Maintain your own gear, uniform and equipment.

- Represent your group in a professional and positive manner.

- Keep your guardian updated as to your whereabouts at all times.

- Be on time.

- Show appreciation to people who have made this trip possible (parents, guardians, tour organizers, coaches, hosts, event officials). Send postcards or letters and buy small gifts to show thanks.

- Do not put yourself or others in compromising or dangerous situations.

- Travel in groups of 3 or more at all times. Never go out alone.

- Do not bring guests onto the sleeping room areas. Meet only in common areas like lobbies or restaurants.

- Do not use other person's items without their advanced permission.

You can draft your own list of necessary rules by meeting with interested youth members. They will usually be stricter than you may have been. Keep the rules brief.

Alcohol, Drugs and the Opposite Sex

Your group's affiliation with a school or club will usually bring on strict rules relating to drinking alcoholic beverages and the use of any drugs. These are especially sensitive issues if you travel out of the country. In Europe, for example, the attitudes towards minors having an occasional beer, or wine with dinner are very different than what we find in the US. Your destination and itinerary may expose your youth members to this more casual philosophy. Have your planning committee set the expectations and put them in your rules.

For our groups, we have an immediate "no tolerance" policy for any drugs. But for alcohol, we request that players traveling without a parent have a signed Alcohol Release Form (Appendix B5) if the parents agree to let their son or daughter have limited access to beer or wine. The guardian is still expected to monitor their charges for abuse. The signed form is not a carte blanche allowing a drinking binge. The younger the players, the less likely it will be that the parent would sign the form. If no signed form is on file with us (and a copy with the guardian), the player cannot partake at all. If the parents are with the player, it is their call and their responsibility.

In addition to discussing the alcohol/drug issues with all members of the group, we also cover that the focus on this trip is specific and does not include time for romance–at all! Young men and young ladies are not to be in each other's sleeping rooms, are never to be alone together anywhere (See our "Travel in groups of 3 or more" discussion in Chapter 1—*The Game Plan*), and this policy includes people that we encounter along the trip. It is fine for our youth to mix with others during the trip, but not with the intention of finding romance. The guardians are to enforce this policy—no form required.

Your Tour Company/Travel Agent

We have been fortunate to do business with a very professional tour operator. They can make or break your trip. If you have used a travel agent or tour company, they probably have handled transportation, lodging and ground transportation details. Make sure that you have, in writing, what they have agreed to provide, and in what time frame. When do you get your travel tickets, lodging vouchers and tournament/event packets? Who are your contacts at various points along your journey? What do you do if there is an emergency like a transportation strike or flight cancellation? Professional agents will have provided you with literature detailing most of these scenarios, but if not, inquire.

When we travel with groups, we always keep copies of important tour agent correspondence with us. Ours has listed local phone numbers and contact names for our destinations. These have been invaluable on several occasions.

Upon arriving at the Paris airport to catch our flight home, we were informed that the computers had crashed and no one could check in. I had saved an email listing all 50 of our group with their names, 10 digit identifier numbers, and seating assignments. Once I presented this to the airline desk crew, we were issued boarding passes on Post–It notes and proceeded to the boarding gate.

That information allowed them to develop a plan to process and load all 200 passengers. As a thank you, three of us got moved up to first class. I normally would not have "moved up" and left the group, but the coaches and parents said that we never would have left Paris if I had not had that e-mail. The airline staff obviously agreed. The moral is, save key documents and bring them on the trip.

Other requests that we have made were having a representative meet us as we depart our transportation at our destination. Sometimes these representatives must wait just outside security checkpoints, but they can hold a sign with your group's name and you will connect. They then can lead your entourage to the ground transportation. This person is very important when traveling in areas where language may pose a challenge, or where the ground transportation is located far from the airport or train station. And if not in the US, your driver may not speak enough English to understand your needs.

Tour company representatives can also aid with the lodging, whether it is home stays, hotels or dorms. They are local and can give you insights that you won't find on the internet. If there are initial problems upon move-in, they represent "future" business and the lodging staff is more likely to accommodate your needs if reasonable.

We had landed in Milan with four teams, gathered our luggage and gone through the Italian customs, and as we exited into the airport lobby, we did not see anyone to greet us and guide us to the buses. We waited quite a while thinking that someone was going to arrive, but I decided to walk around and see if I could find any bus lots.

A good 200 yards outside the airport, and after trying to use my "lame French" with the Italians, I finally found a bus with our name on the window. The driver was napping soundly. When I woke him, he pointed to the airport and gestured, "Come now." I decided it was better to bring the group to him rather than try to explain where the group was waiting.

The moral here is to make arrangements for a representative with a sign standing where you exit the customs or other secured arrival area. This is a reasonable request and makes the transition out of the airport much more pleasant.

For tours that may have been included, you may need to confirm arrival times and if voucher proof is needed. And also ask if there are restrictions at the tour location, such as women must cover their heads, no shorts can be worn, no cameras allowed, no sleeveless dresses, or no sandals can be worn. They can also give you a current update on what you will see on that tour.

Part of our itinerary on one of our trips was to visit an art museum near the village of St. Paul de Vence. The travel museum stated that the museum hosts rotating collections of contemporary French art and sculpture. We had to walk up a very steep hill (almost killing some of the parents), and pay individually (which took forever). I was greatly relieved when we were all inside the courtyard gate and we proceeded into the museum. To my shock, the current exhibit was "Nudes of the 1920's and 1930's." This was not the experience that I was seeking for our soccer families. Although the exhibit was modern art and abstract, it still was a surprise.

The lesson here is plan for such visits. A day or so ahead, check into what type of art is currently on exhibit, how you can pay one group fee, and how far and difficult the walk from the bus is. My group took the experience in stride and we headed for the beaches to recover.

For tours that are not included, I suggest collecting the fee in advance so you can buy the tickets as a group with a discounted price. Sometimes you can put the group fees on your credit card and then have the members reimburse you. Also, ask for student rates.

The technology that cell phones has provided makes traveling so much simpler. For your home cell, you can expand your zones of coverage for the trip period and at your destination. This allows you to easily connect with your representatives and other group members without having to seek out a phone booth. When you have more than one bus, walkie-talkies help you keep in touch without expensive cell phone use. Walkie-talkies can also prove to be useful if staying at different but nearby hotels.

Once at your destination, you will most likely be using ground transportation to get around. Some groups will charter their own buses. This gives you more control and greater flexibility. Remember that drivers can only work so many hours per day, must have rest and meal breaks, and will respond well when you show them your appreciation with a small gift like a baseball cap or polo shirt. It is important to exchange cell phone numbers and to verify your itinerary with your driver. Discuss any changes that are needed, and ask if it will affect the cost to your group (if arranged by your tour agent, a fixed budget is already in place). Ask what rules the driver may have on the bus: no eating, no drinking, no feet on the seats, restroom...a must for long trips...and video availability. Drivers are very territorial about their bus. They are very proud of them and maintain them well, and in Europe, many drivers own their own bus.

A good driver, if treated with respect, will bend over backwards to do small favors and offer little perks to you group. For long commutes during these trips, we've had drivers share their videos with the passengers. The monitors on board turn your bus into a movie theater. We have also enjoyed seeing American films in the local language. We laughed so hard that it hurt watching "Mr. Bean" in Italian and "Titanic" and "Men in Black" were easy to follow in French. Drivers have also been known to open up their beverage bar. That is a nice touch for the group!

We have always treated our drivers with appreciation and respect. They have reciprocated by being flexible and 'going the extra mile' for us..

Some tournaments/competitions provide shuttle services. Find out what restrictions there may be. If you have a large group, can you all fit? Are other groups using the shuttles at the same time period as your group? Does the schedule fit your itinerary? If not, what alternatives does your group have (City transportation? Walk?).

Again, if you run into major problems, involve the local representative from your tour operator if you used one. If not, contact the company office and speak to a manager. Be polite, but firm with your concerns and your needs.

Lodging Management
And What YOU need from them.

What's Included

Before you leave on your trip, you should have details on where your group will be staying. You will have already evaluated whether home-stays, dorms or hotels were the best fit for your youth group. With that in place, you would want to know some of the basics to prepare your members and minimize disappointments.

When traveling in North America, we have come to expect that our lodging will provide bedding (pad, sheets, blanket, pillows, towels) and certain little amenities like in-room restrooms/showers, small soaps, shampoo, hair dryers, TV's, swimming pools and ice machines. Even if staying on our home continent, it is not a bad idea to inquire as to these items. It makes packing easier.

But when you travel abroad (Europe, Asia, etc) everything changes unless you are staying in four-star hotels (which, with the cost, is not likely). These niceties that we take for granted will probably not be provided. With the assistance of a good tour operator, or if you made the arrangements yourself, an email or call can clear up any confusion and help you prepare your members. We enjoy the differences between lodging in Europe and here in the US. It makes us feel like we've been someplace special. But those differences may be a surprise to your group. **Remember to ask about these little items when you make you lodging arrangements.**

> When we arrived in Chioggia, Italy in 2002, we knew that the hotels would not have air conditioning. We therefore sent the boosters out to scout the neighborhood for a grocery store and a small appliance store. Both were nearby and we stocked up on box and table fans, shampoo and bottled water. If we hadn't asked questions of the hotel owner in advance, we would not have been prepared with our solution.

A typical adapter for an outlet in Italy.

More Questions For Lodging Management

(Remember that there are NO stupid questions!)

- If you have a group gift for the manager/owner, ask when they can join you all for this presentation (start with this one. It will set THEIR mood for answering your other questions and accommodating your needs)

- Does the site lock their doors at a particular time of night, and if so, how do you get back in, or exit?

- What is the emergency plan for a fire? Where are the exits? Where are the alarm levers to alert everyone?

- Are the power outlets standard for that region?

- Do the rooms or front desk have a security safe? Is it free? How do you use it? What hours do you have access?

- Does the hot water stop at certain times of the evening?

- What areas are air-conditioned?

- How do the room ventilators/heaters work?

- Do all the windows in the rooms open? If so, how?

- What sections of the hotel are the quietest?

- Do you have to return the room key to the front desk when going out of the hotel?

- If meals are included, where and what time will your group eat? Is the menu a buffet, served or a combination? What courses are served first? Where do diners obtain beverages? (served at the table? From a table or bar? Served in courses? Pay as you go or free or tab?)

- If your itinerary makes you miss a mealtime, can you prearrange an alternative mealtime? Can they provide a sack or boxed to-go meal?

- Does the site have a laundromat? If not, where is the nearest one?

- Where is the nearest grocery/sundries store?

- Where is the nearest bank or currency exchange kiosk?

- Where can you make calls? Calls to another country? How much are these calls.

- Where can you buy postcard stamps?

- Are there areas nearby that should be avoided by your group?

- Where can you hold group meetings that are private and will not disturb other guests? And where can you post any updates (don't post in areas open to the general public). We have posted updates on the room door of the group leader and the coaches/bandleaders/trainers.

- Where are the closest spaces for practices? Nearby parks? Schools?

A bidet in a European bathroom may confuse some youth members...it is not a baby bathtub!

It may be possible to send some of these questions ahead before you leave on your trip thus giving you some of the answers early.

Many lessons have been learned on our trips. Most have a funny story. Here are four that emphasize the points made above.

1.   In Verona, we tried to exit our hotel early one morning to catch the 5:30 AM train to Florence. We were literally locked in. Even the exits marked as "Fire Exits" were chained shut once the desk staff goes home late at night. We "escaped" through one fire door whose lock had been left open. Speak to your hotel about emergencies as well as unusual leave and arrival times. We have always been given a different key to help these situations.

2.   Arriving about 10:30 AM at our Amsterdam hotel after an all-night flight, we were told that we could not get room keys until after 2:00–3:00 PM. We had not known this at the time and had no plan for getting people out sightseeing and locking up the luggage. Since then, we plan our arrival times with itinerary that matches the access to the hotel rooms. Keep this in mind during your planning phase at home.

3.   Meals are one of the many joys of traveling. We love to try the new foods, tastes, smells and local specialties. But the order of dinner, number of courses and other etiquette may be different than home. We went to our first dinner in Montecatini, Italy, had salad from a salad bar, then a great pasta dish. Thinking that was it, many of the 120 members began to leave to walk around the town. The waiters began running around the dining room yelling "secondi, secondi" that meant nothing to us. The hotel manager came up and explained that there was a second course, then dessert and coffee as well. We then gathered up the group again and continued with a great dinner.

4.   In the next hotel on that same trip, we headed for the salad bar first and were chastised in Italian for some "faux pas." We were clueless until an Australian couple explained that here in this hotel they eat salad the way most Europeans do...at the end of the meal. Once educated, we were fine.

Put someone in charge of clarifying these simple details to help the group acclimate to the culture a bit easier.

Most older European hotels have very large, bulky keys. This is to discourage you from taking them. When you leave a hotel for a stroll or for dinner, you usually give your key to the front desk.

Tournament/Event Organizer

As your youth group is traveling to participate in some activity, there will be someone from the host city organizing those details. Many of those details may be sent to you in advance. Read through the literature carefully and ask questions when things are not clear or complete. Find out exactly what they need from you and your group. Whether it is a tournament, performance or competition, your host may need documentation like player cards, personal ID, birth certificates, group/team rosters, proof of health insurance coverage, official travel papers, etc.

You will need to know locations, maps and written directions with drive times, schedules with times, inclement weather restrictions, special event specifics, and site limitations such as small stages, lack of locker rooms, or no food/beverage service. Asking ahead saves disappointment.

Show your appreciation to them with some type of gift presented in front of your group and their staff. Again, this sets the mood for their treatment of you.

Hosting a major athletic event is a big deal for any city throughout the world. The smaller the city, the bigger the deal. The bigger the deal, the more "important" are the organizers and hosts. A few nice gestures upon your arrival will put your group in with the "privileged" few. In our gifts chapter we speak about taking lots of items with us to give out and show our appreciation for the efforts made by these locals to produce the event. We've made the front cover of the local newspaper while presenting a gift basket to the local mayor or a polo shirt from our team to the tournament director. They are not used to American treating them like this, and they love it. It makes your groups impressive ambassadors from your region, and will open many doors to your members that may not have been possible before.

Team Seattle Newspaper Clips

Contributed photo

Chapter 9

The Trip

After months of planning, meetings, fundraisers, recruiting and phone calls, it is finally time to go. When we begin planning our trips 10 to 18 months in advance, it seems like we have an eternity to get ready. But it is frightening how fast the time passes. In this section, we discuss that actual trip. There may be some repetition of details, but they are worth highlighting.

Travel Folders

A few weeks before the trip, we produce and distribute a "Traveler Folder" to each member family. These folders contain a wealth of information. Each traveler is encouraged to carry it with them at all times. It contains information such as:

- The travel group roster

- The flight schedule

- Airplane etiquette

- Airport maps

- The packing list

- Hotel names, addresses, phone numbers, faxes and emails

- The general itinerary

- A calendar with the month/s traveled

- Vicinity maps where you stay

- Language tips with simple sayings

- Short articles about sightseeing destinations

- Brief behavior tips for airport security, pedestrian rules in the areas you'll visit, taboos of that culture (pointing, spitting), appropriate attire for some areas (churches may require sleeves and no shorts)

This folder is very important if the travelers gets separated from the group and need help finding their way back. This may be another project for one of your parent "volunteers."

What to Pack

Most groups will have a wide variety of "packers." Some members will take what they are wearing and 3 pairs of underwear, while others may wish to bring their entire wardrobe. You must first find out what baggage restrictions are enforced by your airline, train or bus. Most have strict limits on the number of bags, the size of those bags (height, length, width) and the maximum weight of each bag. You should then decide whether or not to add other limitations. We have allowed 1 check-in bag and a carry-on bag.

With that defined, we suggest giving your travelers a packing list. We have a sample packing list in **Appendix D**. You will see that we list more than just clothes. The youth member's baggage must be checked for compliance by his or her trip guardian before departing from home. And remember... leave room for souvenirs!

To better identify our members' luggage, backpacks, team bags and camera bags, we have always issued hot pink ribbon that they are all to affix to the handles or straps. This is of great help for security reasons. If a stranger is walking off with one of our items with this ribbon attached, you can more easily notice it. It is also much easier and quicker to spot when coming down the luggage chute in a crowded airport. When you arrive at a destination and are claiming your luggage, you just have all ribboned luggage pulled aside and then you sort it out.

Departure Tips

Just getting to airport, train station or bus pickup point can be a challenge (See Appendix E—Team Seattle Travel Tips). One late member will often delay the entire group from checking in. A power outage or misset alarm clock can mean disaster. For this reason, we set up phone trees for wake/pick up calls to all members. Key trip organizers start the process by calling several adult members who in turn filter the process on to all members. As carpools are common, drivers contact their riders as part of the phone tree.

We pad the suggested arrival time of the transportation agency by 60 minutes. This has saved us when important items like a ticket or passport have been left at home, and someone has to run them down to us. Also remind members that if they keep such documents in their bank safety deposit box, they need to get them out two business days or more beforehand.

Having the members wear a travel shirt will help you identify them in crowded areas. It also helps transportation staff to identify your group.

Have guardians match up with their charges, and visibly check required travel necessities like:

- Photo ID (student card, driver's license, passport)

- Birth certificate

- Plane, train or bus ticket

- Spending money (cash, traveler's checks, debit or credit cards)

> At check-in, one of our coaches was pulled aside when his carry-on was found to contain a large pocketknife. Despite his lectures to the players, he had missed this knife in his bag's end pocket. He explained to security that he used the knife to cut the tape holding the goal netting to the frames. They did not care and searched every inch of his bag, clothing, and shoes before sending him on his way. Yes, they kept the knife.

At another check-in for a flight from Holland to Spain, a player who was under our guardianship was pulled aside by security forces after his carry-on bag was screened. When the bag was opened, security pulled out what looked like a small handgun. The player was immediately taken out of our sight into a side room. We were frantic, but at least the Dutch security spoke English. All of our group ceased boarding the plane and waited. A few minutes later the player came back out with his bag and a very frightened look. Security explained to us that what appeared to look like a handgun was actually a cigarette lighter. Security waved us on and the trip proceeded.

Then have the guardians do a carry-on bag check looking for prohibited items or things that resemble them:

- Firearms, knives, Swiss Army knives, pointed scissors or nail files
- Duct or strapping tape
- Flammables or explosives like fireworks or cigarette lighter fuel
- Spray paint or adhesive
- Items prohibited at your destination (chewing gum, certain magazines, or political symbols like swastikas).

Carrying any banned items, such as fireworks, aerosol cans or knives into foreign countries can cause trouble for the entire group.

Once your group is assembled, you should have check-in instructions from attending staff that your point-person sought out earlier. Follow their instructions and organize you group either alphabetically by last name, in family groups, or with guardians. Agree on where to meet or wait once members have checked in. Assign one of the first adults through the check-in as "tender of the flock" to organize the team after they get through security.

If passing through security checkpoints is part of the plan for passengers, alert your members to be serious and to not make jokes. This will slow the group down if a member is pulled aside unnecessarily. The guardian should always be just behind his or her charge/s. This prevents the guardian from being on the wrong side of a barricade if one of their 'trip kids' happen to get singled out. If so, alert security that the youth's guardian wishes to be present during the check.

Proceed to the holding areas and keep members aware of how much time they have before boarding. If hungry, thirsty or in need of a restroom break, tell the guardians to have their charges arrive at the specified point at least ten minutes early. Keep an eye on their carry–on bags. The ribbon mentioned earlier is helpful, but if a bag is left under a seat or in a restroom, that ribbon is the first thing a thief will cut off. Then that bag looks just like thousands of others.

Boarding/Loading and Unloading

When it is time to board, assign someone to be the last of your group out of your waiting area. They are to look for items left behind that might belong to someone in the group.

If you have assigned seats, the boarding is simple. For those members who want to trade seats, let them proceed on their own. Try not to get involved or you'll find yourself becoming the seat monitor for the rest of the trip. But if trades are being considered, make sure that it is equitable for all involved, but have guardians play a big role in such situations. Don't sacrifice youth members into a bad seating arrangement just because they are too shy or soft–spoken to stand up for themselves. Depending on the length of your trip, most of us can be flexible and roll with the punches. But there are instances where individuals will take advantage of others. Watch for this and only interfere if necessary.

If seating is not assigned, as on most buses, be watchful that all youth members are seated in the same areas. There is nothing worse for most young people than to have to sit with the adults. Make sure that the space you have is divided reasonably between the youth group and the adults. Watch out for individuals who hog a double or triple seat for themselves, making others squeeze into what is left. If seating is limited, be specific when boarding where larger carry–on bags, sports bags, instruments are to be stowed. If on a bus, these can be carefully packed below, and it will give everyone in the passenger compartment much more room.

With few basic guidelines, everyone will be happy with the seating arrangements and this helps create opportunities for other fun time.

In Transit

While you are in transit, be sensitive to the members' desire to congregate and the impact on other travelers. Conversations help to pass the time, but if your members are keeping others awake, or blocking aisles or views of the movie screen, try to move those members to a more suitable location. This is just a courtesy that reasonable travelers practice.

Remember that this may be the first trip for some of your members. We've had members who had never flown before, or have never traveled outside their home state. A few advanced guidelines will benefit everyone. Let them know these types of travel hints:

- What on–board meals will be served? (Hot entrée's with a choice, sandwiches, snacks?) Is there a cost for these meals?

- What beverages are included and which ones cost? Usually the alcoholic beverages are the ones that cost you, so the minors will not be offered these anyway.

- Are the headphones used to watch the in–flight movies free or rented for a fee? How much do these cost? Encourage members to have lots of one–dollar bills.

- Program channels may be in more than one language.

- The on–board phones are very expensive.

- Always lock the restroom door after entering.

- Pillows and blankets are available

- There are times during flights that CD or DVD players cannot be used.

While on board, we have regularly sent a note up to the pilot or driver introducing our group as representing our school, home town, state or country at the destination event. A welcome and good luck announcement is oftentimes made and that is a big deal to the youth members. Other travelers will many times step forward and offer wishes of luck and congratulations.

Disembarking

When you disembark, make a final check of all seat and overhead storage. We have left enough clothes and souvenirs to stock a warehouse. This will save your members a lot of disappointments. Have one adult lead the group with one behind it. Rendezvous as soon as possible to give instructions for transfers, baggage claim/unloading, and security/customs checkpoints. If unsure of what to do next or where to go, ask one of the employees as you exit the plane, bus or train. Don't lead your group on a wild goose chase. When you still don't know where to go next, have one or two of your boosters scout out the area and return with their findings. Then lead the group onward.

If you have had a long trip, some of the group may need to use a restroom. It is our recommendation to take the entire group to the restroom area and wait until all that need to use it have done so.

A Typical scene on checkout at one of our hotels. Tagging the luggage with the owner's ID and the pink ribbon have made retrieval go smoothly at our destinations.

When you get to the point to reclaim your luggage, regardless if it is from under your bus or at the baggage carousel, assign several of your stronger members to pull the luggage out to a central point. Just looking for the pink ribbon has made this simple for our group. Once the baggage is pulled, sort it out and make sure everyone had his or her bags.

If anything is missing, most airports and train stations have a "lost luggage" office where you fill out a report. Your baggage claim check is very important. Give them all the numbers from the claim check, but keep it until you get the bag. Also let them know where you are going to be staying and they will often deliver the bags there. If the bag is missing for several days, most airlines will give you a small allotment to buy some replacement clothes. Keep ALL receipts. If the missing luggage belongs to a youth member, make sure that the guardian is involved. This is not time well–spent for the group leader.

The Move–In

When arriving at hotel–type lodging, we recommend sending your group leader or one of your friendly boosters inside to check–in with the front desk. Keep the group outside (unless weather is bad) until that person has scoped out the lobby, received the update on room availability (are the rooms ready yet?), and other pertinent news.

We then suggest that three adults visit every room that has been assigned to your group. Evaluate how many each room will house, where are the quiet areas and the noisy areas, and how best to organize your group and take notes on a scratch pad. It has proven successful for us to intermix booster rooms in the same area as their charge's rooms, but we do favor the quietest of these rooms for the boosters, as it seems the younger members can sleep through anything. If at a hotel, keep in mind the location of the cocktail lounge, disco and banquet spaces. These tend to be busy and noisy late at night. Check out the neighborhood as well, looking for these same noise sources. You will learn to value your sleep time enormously.

Our tour agent usually has let us know how many double rooms, triples and quads we will have at each site. This allows us to preplan roommates. As your coaches and bandleaders may see a different side of the youth members that you as a parent may see, involve them in matching up the roommates. On our Membership Information Form (Appendix B1), we ask for the top 3 roommate preferences. We state that we try to give them at least one of their choices. *Give a copy of the master rooming list to the front desk and to key boosters.*

Once you have your room assignment plan in place, remind the guardians to do the room check of their charge's rooms. Then, if elevator space is limited, give priority to those members with rooms on the upper floors. Have members with second or third–floor rooms use the stairs if possible.

Elevators in many
older foreign
hotels will be small,
with the capacity
for 2 or 3 people
without luggage.

For dorm stays, many of these tips will apply. The facilities may be more limited and more spartan. Shared bathrooms and showers are common.

When using home–stays, your tour company's land contact will have all the information and let you know what is provided and what you need to pack. This is a wonderful way to live with the locals and really experience their culture. Such experiences are exciting to some young people, but intimidating to others. Pairing your youth members may help ease this concern.

Before the group separates to go to their rooms, let them know what and when the next group rendezvous will be (for meals, meetings, practices, tours). Once dispersed, it may be difficult to pass on this important detail.

When in Rome…

Once the group has had time to get settled in, encourage the members to get out for a walk or jog. Some coaches have taken the players out for a run. Getting some fresh air and acclimating to the change in any new time zones is important. In some cases, you may be 8 or more hours different than at home. Adapting quickly to the schedule of the locals will make the trip much more enjoyable. During the first day or two, suggest short catnaps if the itinerary allows. Also allow for a good nights sleep the first night or two.

After check–in, get the group outside to get them acclimated to the local time zone.

Send your scouts out into the community to bring back reports to the group on the local sights, and amenities like markets, laundromats or internet cafés. Inquire if there are any local festivals or open markets that may be scheduled during your stay. Meet with your key people, your hosts, guides and drivers and briefly discuss the planned itinerary. Get printed maps and directions to sights, fields and other itinerary locations. We have asked for and received great advice from the locals and have avoided bad choices that seemed like great ones when at home. Remember to be as flexible as possible while keeping the needs of the whole group in mind. Seeing a particular site on one day versus another is not usually a big deal unless you are scheduled with a tournament or performance that day.

Look at the gaps in your days. Do you have several hours between one event and another? If so, suggest to the group that they see a nearby site. Use your time well. These spaces also make good "free time" when the individuals can pursue their own interests. Some members may prefer to see a church or gardens. Others may elect to stroll around the area. You need to keep in mind that the trip will pass very quickly and you want to absorb as much as you can. Even a short trip to the local food store can be interesting as they offer many items not seen at home. We often buy souvenirs at such stores, since food makes great gifts. Regional cookies, candies, cheeses, snack packs, mustards, coffee, tea, spices and even pet food all make unique gifts. Yes, we did say pet foods. Small foil packets of cat food have been well received by relatives and friends with felines in their families. Most of the items above also are small, lightweight and easy to pack on the way home.

Other things to get at such food stores are snacks, beverages, bottled water and fresh fruit to keep the "troops" happy between meals. Our youth groups never seemed to get full no matter how much we fed them at planned meals.

If the youth members did not bring a camera or have used up their film, look for disposable cameras. They are everywhere, easy to use, pack easy for development once home, and even come waterproofed for those pool and beach outings.

Our photo historian captures youth members and boosters
giving directions to the town center in Monaco.

Say Cheese...

Keep your trip historians busy too. The photographer and videographer should be shadowing the members occasionally to compile a good sampling of everyone, not just their own family members. These pictures and video footage will be great for your post trip newsletters and parties. Remind these "artists" to not be shy in setting up or staging shots. And involve the locals and local sights as much as possible. Group shots in front of windmills, Roman ruins or castles are priceless. Make a list of everyone's birthdays and anniversaries available and plan mini–celebrations. Or just plan a get–together with beverages and snacks before dinner. Poolside or rooftop terraces are always nice options if available. These occasions can be used to introduce hosts, guides, hotel management, etc.

On one trip, the first of three flight groups had their schedule changed due to a mechanical problem with the plane. Because of this, they arrived at about 3:00 AM Italy time—this made them 12 hours late. They all arrived in good spirits, pulling their wheeled bags on the cobblestones of Montecatini Terme. That evening we booked the pool terrace at the next hotel and had a pre-dinner reception to officially welcome what became known as the "Lost Tribe." There were no whiners in that group.

Dear Mom and Dad...

Postcard dinners are another hallmark of our trips. We want the members, especially the youth members, to show their appreciation to their family back home. We have them write at least one post card (more is better) and bring it to dinner. We have stamps available for purchase from a willing booster, and then put all the post cards into a basket. We then draw one or two of the postcards and give out door prizes. This rewards all those who participated. And we require youth members traveling without a parent to participate. They are usually very willing to do so once nudged. We will do about two of these postcard dinners per week of travel. These cards and letters to parents, grandparents, siblings, friends and teachers mean so much and require the members to give some reflection about the trip.

The Daily Gazette

We have mentioned before that posting a daily update on your itinerary is of great benefit. No matter how much information you have supplied to your members, they will constantly be asking, "When do we leave for…?" "What time is…?" "How do I know where to…" Having details posted in a central spot accessible to just your group is invaluable. Don't post this in the common areas of hotels or dorms, as you do not want to have strangers aware of your comings and goings. We usually post it on one boosters room door per floor. We never post rooming assignments, but do provide many copies of that list to key boosters and one behind the front hotel desk. This keeps that information available but confidential from anyone outside your group.

Daily Journals

Over the years we have had several of our youth members keep a daily travel journal. The contents can reflect their thoughts on the day's activities and detail historical and cultural facts that were learned. Besides being a great souvenir source, journals have been used to satisfy summer school requirements or credit in upcoming classes like history, art, foreign languages or political science.

Hungry tour group members sit down for dinner in Cesenatico, Italy.

Mealtimes

Mealtimes when eating as a group can go smoothly with a little research. Share how the meal will be served with your group. Don't assume that everyone around the world eats dinner the same way you do. Is the meal buffet or served, or a combination? What are the courses and in what order? If you want more, is it polite to ask for seconds? How are beverages served? Is there a cost?

These types of questions should have been asked of the lodging staff upon your arrival. If this information is shared with your group, there will be no surprises. Your youth members may feel very self-conscious in these situations. It is up to the group leaders, guides and other boosters to explain how things work, and to set the example. Even attire may be worthy of clarification. Some dining rooms prohibit shorts and swimwear. Dinner attire may be even more formal, requiring men to wear long pants and women to wear dresses or skirts.

Wasting food is also discouraged in most countries. If the meal is buffet, let members know to only take what they can eat. And it is usually discouraged to take any food out of the dining room.

> At one hotel, meals were buffet-style, with one rule—"no food could be taken out of the dining room." One booster was late boarding the bus for a sightseeing tour and also had not been able to eat lunch. So he grabbed a few rolls from the buffet and headed for the bus. Chased by the Maître d', the booster ran into and broke a glass door, luckily getting only a few cuts. As I arrived, the rolls were being thrown at the Maître d', who was cowering behind the front desk, whilst yelling at the top of their lungs. Our guide waged peace between all parties and got the booster patched up. The lesson...follow the rules and don't throw rolls at strangers.

Round 'Em Up, Head 'Em Out...

Regrouping after a game, performance or a local tour can be a challenge. Select a rendezvous location that is easily accessible, visible from a distance, away from crowds and has some cover from sun and weather. Set a strict time to arrive at this location. Make the guardians responsible for their charges as well as for themselves. Stick to your load and leave time. Set the rules up-front and be prompt. Do not punish those members who were on time by waiting for those who are not. Once one bunch misses the bus or train, the word spreads fast to be on time. We have never had any trouble with youth members, but have had a couple boosters who were late and had to find a train to get back to our lodging.

Dividing Up The "Loot"

As discussed in the chapter on Gifts, we bring presents when we leave for a game, performance or reception. As we have gifts to give, we also receive gifts. We handle who keeps each gift depending on whether or not the gift was given to the group or to an individual member. Gifts given person-to-person are kept by the member who receives the gift. This could include a pin, a shirt or a hat. But for gifts given from a group or team to your group or team, a booster or guardian collects the gifts to be given out at the post-trip party. This could include pennants, books, posters or handicrafts. Items like trophies or placement plaques (first place, second place, etc.) need to be decided upon before you leave. School groups would display these at their school, as would a group from a sports club with a clubhouse. If the group is not affiliated with a school or a sports club, the coach or leader may keep them personally. This should be decided ahead of time to avoid any conflicts.

Colorful pennants from tours around the world make great reminders of the wonderful memories of our travels.

From Here to Eternity

While on a trip that involves more than one city, state or country, your hop between one and the other may be a big issue. If the trip takes several hours, do you fly, or take a bus or train? Remember that each time that you regroup, board and disembark is tedious. For this reason and from the wise counsel of our tour operator, we have always used buses when practicable. They meet you at the front door of your lodging of one city and drop you off at the front door of the lodging in the next. No commute to the train station or airport, check in lines, baggage claim, etc. Just door–to–door service. And again, in your planning phase, ask for buses with restrooms.

When moving the group between two cities and the travel time is more than three hours, we do not recommend doing any stops for sightseeing along the way. Meal and restroom stops may be needed, but additional stops usually are not worth the time spent when you look at the whole day. As a rule you need to go through the move–in process again in the next city, and that is time consuming and tiring. Don't pack too many things into these travel days.

If using buses for these city hops, we suggest arranging with your driver to play American movies done with foreign dubbing. As we said earlier, we have seen "Mr. Bean" in Italian, and "Titanic" and "Men In Black" in French. They were hilarious and were huge hits with young and old alike.

For those meal breaks, we will often ask the lodging site to pack up boxes of breads, juices, cheeses, meats and beverages if we are missing a meal that was included. The driver can find a suitable roadside stop and this food can be put out picnic style. Bring out a couple of soccer balls or Frisbees to get people moving around. These stops do not take long and help break up long trips. We have used these videos and picnics to nicely survive 13–hour bus rides in Europe. The bus rides are good times for catching up on your sleep and for seeing the countryside between your destinations.

Chapter 10

Post–Trip Considerations
Thank You, Thank You, Thank You

Don't Forget the Support People

To make your trip possible, many people may have donated time, money or product. All of the people who helped will really appreciate acknowledgement and thanks for their hard work. As with most of us, their time and resources are precious. Depending on the extent of their gift to your group, they may be very happy with a letter or card signed by all, but a gift in return to them may be even better. These can be items purchased on the trip. A city pennant, candy, or polo shirt will all show your appreciation. A letter of thanks listing the value of their contribution can also help their tax breaks too.

People to remember might include:

- Your tour group leader

- Your coach, bandleader or trainer

- Major trip committee heads

- Any sponsors

- The tour operator/travel agent

- The airline/bus contact

Reunions

After each of our trips, we have planned group reunions. We make these casual potlucks and focus on letting people reminisce. Members are notified well in advance of the reunion date. It will often be publicized before we have even left on the trip.

At the reunion, we encourage members to bring their trip albums. It is fun to look at other member's pictures and how they have arranged them in the albums. A contest for the best youth album or adult album might be fun.

We also set up a table for extra loose pictures. We call this the "bring one, take one station." People can easily make an extra set of prints for this and it is fun to supplement your own pictures. It also gives those who are not good photographers a chance to have a few pictures for themselves. This is especially good for youth members who did not take as many shots as their parents would have liked.

Videos are another way to relive the trip. Remember that your members do probably not want to watch many long videos, so keep them short. Either edit the video into a short overview, or just let the video run while people visit. If they wish to watch, they can. We have had video contests between different teams from a trip. We have them make lively music videos less than 5 minutes long. The creative ideas used with today's technology can really be excellent.

Awards are also a fun addition to a reunion. Have group leaders submit one or two awards each pinpointing specific individuals for humorous recognition, such as:

- Messiest Room
- Most likely to miss the bus
- Biggest Suitcase
- Best Interpreter

We print certificates for these winners and make them step forward to receive it. We also receive gifts for our group from other groups that we encounter on our trips. We pool them and do random drawings from a hat to select what member will get the pennant, plaque or trophy. If a gift was of personal nature, we let that person keep it.

Because you probably wont get a 100% attendance with your group, a post-trip newsletter with pictures might be considered. It is a good project for your student members. Copies can be sent to all member families, sponsors, or local media, and it becomes another great memento of the trip.

> Newsletters are a great way to generate excitement about a future
> trip and make wonderful souvenirs of the trip of a lifetime.

Parting Words of Encouragement

We sincerely hope you have enjoyed our travel experiences and stories. We wish you all many wonderful travel adventures either as a participant, booster, or leader. Good Luck! May your trip be a very special adventure to remember and cherish.

Appendices Section

Appendix A

Family Account Excel Files Samples

Conway; Claire, Terry, Adam				
2 Boosters @ $3,050, + Player @ $2,950 = $9,050				
DATE	✓ #	ITEM	AMT	TOTAL
8/14/04	1270	Dep	$600	$600
8/30/04	1284	Pmt	$1,200	$1,800
9/28/04	1301	Pmt	$1,200	$3,000
10/31/04	1327	Pmt	$2,000	$5,000
11/28/04	1355	Pmt	$1,200	$6,200
12/30/04	1371	Pmt	$1,200	$7,400
2/27/05	1402	Pmt	$1,200	$8,600
5/30/05	1475	Final	$450	$9,050

Terrel; Kayla, Nick				
2 Players @ $2,950 = $5,900				
DATE	✓ #	ITEM	AMT	TOTAL
7/31/04	845	Dep	$400	$400
9/1/04	857	Pmt	$800	$1,200
10/1/04	873	Pmt	$800	$2,000
10/30/04	881	Pmt	$800	$2,800
11/27/04	897	Pmt	$800	$3,600
12/29/04	907	Pmt	$800	$4,400
2/28/05	967	Pmt	$800	$5,200
4/30/05	941	Pmt	$400	$5,650
5/28/05	994	Final	$350	$5,950

Appendix B

Cover Letter

August 22, 2003

Dear Kayla, Ann and Doug:

We are very happy to have Kayla as part of our Team Seattle 2004 adventure. It's shaping up to be as wonderful as our past trips. We received your $200.00 deposit and will credit that against the player package cost of $2950.00. Kayla will be on the Girl's 1986 team.

We have enclosed several forms. Please look them over and feel free to call me if you have any questions. **Mail enrollment forms to Ann Terrel.**

- The Team Seattle Member Information Form (white): One per traveler. Complete this form with as much current information as possible. Use **legal names as they appear on your passport**. Do not worry about uniform sizes or roommates as you can call those in later. We will have sample uniforms here in September for you to try on. And as you learn who else has joined our group, you can call in your roommate preferences. I try to match up players with at least one of their choices.

- Minor Release Form (yellow): To be filled out for players under 19, signed by parents before a notary and notarized.

- Player Medical Release Form (white): To be filled out for players under 19, signed by parents before a notary and notarized. Coaches/group leaders use this when parents aren't at the game and there is an injury.

- Behavior for Team Seattle Members (green): Two page listing of our behavior code.

- Agreement of Behavior (goldenrod): One per traveler. Sign this agreement after reading the green Behavior Code.

- Alcohol Consumption Release (pink): To be completed for minors under 21 IF the parent/s wish to allow the minor to drink alcoholic beverages while in Europe.

Please complete the above forms, make copies for your self, and **return the originals to us as soon as possible.**

We also **strongly** encourage you to enroll in the Travel Guard trip insurance. Their website is www.Travelguard.Com. Use Euro-Sportring as the "Tour Operator", Northwest/KLM as the "Airline", and as the "Date of Initial Trip Payment", use any week date the week you sign up. Call Mary Kay with questions. You should do this now.

- We also would like 4 legal sized self-addressed, stamped envelopes for mailings.

- We would like monthly payments in the amount of $275.00.

First payment is due October 1st and last before June 1st, 2004.

Late payments cost us penalties. For other arrangements or questions, contact Mary Kay. Make all checks out to **Team Seattle.** We are looking forward to knowing you better through this great trip.

Best regards,

Appendix B1

Member Information Form

TEAM SEATTLE

MEMBER INFORMATION FORM
Please Print

Trip Package (Booster, Player): _____ Deviation: Yes or No.
NAME: First:_____ Last _____
PHONE: Home_____-_____-_____ Work_____-_____-_____
E-Mail:_____ Fax:_____
Home Address:_____City:_____Zip:_____
Player Parents: Mother _____Same Address? Y or N
                    Father _____Same Address? Y or N
Alternate Address: _____City:_____Zip_____
Alternate Phone: _____
TRAVELER MEDICAL: List Allergies/Medications _____
_____Date of Last Tetanus_____
TRIP PACKAGE: _____ Standard July 18th, 2004 – July 31st, 2005
                         _____ Deviation _____
Tee Shirt Size (all adult** sizes, circle 1): Sm Med Lg XLg XXLg

PLAYER INFORMATION:
Birthdate: _____/_____/_____ Current School: _____
Trip Guardian: _____ Same Trip Package? Y or N
Club Age Group: B or G/U _____ Club Team: _____
Club Team Coach: _____
Club Name _____
Positions Played _____
Uniform Sizes (**all adult** sizes, circle 1 each; will have samples)
   Jersey: Sm   Med   Lg   XLg   XXLg   *Shorts:* Sm   Med   Lg   XLg
3 Favorite Jersey #'s: _____ _____ _____
3 Roommate Preferences: _____
_____
_____

Office Use Only:
_____ Orientation   _____ Passport Copy   _____ Drinking Release
_____ Medical Release   _____ Team Seattle Release   _____ Deviation Form
                          _____ Behavior   _____ Guardianship

TEAM SEATTLE
teamseattle@comcast.net
www.teamseattle.info

Appendix B2-a

Minor Release Form

I/we hereby agree that my/our son/daughter, _____'s participation in soccer competition carries with it a potential hazard. I/we hereby release and hold harmless TEAM SEATTLE, its team coaches, group leaders and chaperones from any and all liability in the event of injury during the 2005 European soccer trip from July 18, 2005 through July 31, 2005.

I/we hereby agree that Mary Kay and Larry French are the designated TEAM SEATTLE group leaders. I/we acknowledge and accept that as group and tour leaders, Mary Kay and Larry French are authorized to advise me/us of any breach by my son/daughter of the soccer tournament rules, regulations, codes and/or customs recognized by the host country. Should my son/daughter breach any of these rules, regulations, code or customs, I agree and accept that my son/daughter may be suspended from tournament play and/or sent home at my/our expense. In addition, I/we agree and accept that Mary Kay French and Larry French are all empowered to enforce the Agreement of Behavior for TEAM SEATTLE members.

_____
Print Name

_____
Sign Name

SUBSCRIBED AND SWORN to before me this _____ day of _____ , _____ (year)

By _____
   Signature

and _____
    Signature

_____
Print Name
NOTARY PUBLIC in and for the State of Washington residing at _____
_____

My commission expires: _____

Appendix B2-b

Traveler Release Form

I hereby agree that my participation in the TEAM SEATTLE tour group carries with it a potential hazard. I hereby release and hold harmless TEAM SEATTLE, its team coaches, group leaders and chaperones from any and all liability in the event of injury during the 2005 European soccer trip from July 18, 2005 through July 31, 2005.

I hereby agree that Mary Kay French and Larry French are the designated TEAM SEATTLE group leaders and the designated tour leaders. Mary Kay French, and Larry French are authorized to advise me of any breach of rules, regulations, codes and/or customs recognized by the host country. In addition, I agree and accept that Mary Kay French and Larry French are empowered to enforce the Agreement of Behavior for TEAM SEATTLE Members.

_____
Print Name

SUBSCRIBED AND SWORN to before me this _____ **day of** _____, _____ **(year)**

By _____
Signature

_____
Print Name

NOTARY PUBLIC in and for the State of Washington, residing at _____

_____

My Commission expires: _____

Appendix B3

Parental Guardianship Form

TEAM SEATTLE
PARENTAL GUARDIANSHIP AND TRAVEL AUTHORIZATION
(print clearly)

I/We,_____, the
Parent(s)/Legal Guardian of our daughter/son, _____, give
my/our permission for _____, or any Team Seattle
2005 representative, to seek medical, legal or other help and care on behalf of our
daughter/son during the team trip from July 18th, 2005 to July 31st, 200 to Italy and the
Netherlands, and connections to and from Seattle. During that period, _____
_____ has agreed to be the Guardian(s) and shall have the same parental rights and
responsibilities during that time as I/we do. Other Team Seattle representatives who may
share in this duty may include coaches, trainers, team managers, tour guides or other
appointed adults over the age of 21.
I/we understand that I/we are responsible for costs that may occur above any insurance
coverage.
Our home address is :_____

_____

Our home telephone number in the US is:_____

_____
Son/Daughter's Name (printed)

_____
Parent Name (printed)

_____
Parent Name (printed)
SUBSCRIBED AND SWORN to before me on this _____ day of _____, 2004

By_____
Parent SIGNATURE

By_____
Parent SIGNATURE

Notary Seal here   _____
Notary's Name (printed)

NOTARY PUBLIC in and for the State of Washington residing at_____

_____
Notary's Signature
Updated10-04   My commission expires on:_____

Appendix B4

Medical Release Form

MEDICAL RELEASE FORM

As the parent/legal guardian of _____, I request that in my absence the above-named player be admitted to any hospital or medical facility for diagnosis and treatment. I request and authorize physicians, dentists, and staff, duly licensed as Doctors of Medicine or Doctors of Dentistry or other such licensed technicians or nurses, to perform any diagnostic procedures, treatment procedures, operative procedures and x-ray treatment of the above-named minor. I have not been given a guarantee as to the results of examination or treatment. I authorize the hospital or medical facility to dispose of any specimen or tissue taken from the above-named player.

Date of Player's Birth _____/_____/_____   Date of last Tetanus Booster _____/_____/_____
                       Month Day Year   Month Day Year

Known allergies of this player, including any allergies to medicine
_____

Any other medical problems which should be noted _____
_____

Family Physician _____ Phone ( ) _____ – _____

Name of Parent/Guardian _____
Address _____
City/State/Zip _____
Phone (H) ( ) _____ – _____ (W) ( ) _____ – _____ (FAX) ( ) _____ – _____

Person responsible for charges (if different from above) _____
Address _____
City/State/Zip _____
Phone (H) ( ) _____ – _____ (W) ( ) _____ – _____ (FAX) ( ) _____ – _____

Person to notify if parent/guardian is unavailable _____
Address _____
City/State/Zip _____
Phone (H) ( ) _____ – _____ (W) ( ) _____ – _____ (FAX) ( ) _____ – _____

Insurance Carrier _____ Policy Number _____

Signature of Parent/Guardian _____

STATE OF _____

COUNTY OF _____

Sworn to and subscribed before me on the _____ day of _____ 20_____

Notary Signature _____

Notary Public in and for the State of _____

Commission Expires _____

Appendix B5

Alcohol Release Form

ALCOHOL CONSUMPTION
RELEASE FORM

I, _____, release the coaches and group
Parent/Guardian Name(s) \

leaders of TEAM SEATTLE from any and all consequences of drinking

alcoholic beverages by my daughter/son,_____
Daughter's/Son's Name

_____, while in the supervision of TEAM SEATTLE. I also
understand that if, in the judgement of the coaches, my daughter/son has
drunk excessively to the point of self-endangerment or endangerment or
disruption to the team or travel group, my daughter/son will be returned to
their trip guardian for the remainder of the trip. Guardians have the right to
send the daughter/son back to the States at the parents' expense.

Date:_____   _____
Parent/Guardian Signature

Date:_____   _____
Parent/Guardian Signature

UPDATED 10-04

Appendix B6-a

Agreement of Behavior For Team Seattle Members

1.   BASIC RULE: Group leaders have the final say on all decisions relating to TEAM SEATTLE. Coaches have the final say on all decisions when players are in the supervision of the coaches. Parents/guardians have the final say when "minor-aged" members are under the supervision of those parents/guardians.

2.   General Behavior: It is expected that general behavior of all members of TEAM SEATTLE will be at the highest level. We believe everyone on this trip has already demonstrated a high level of self-control and sportsmanship, players and non-players alike. However, we recognize that we will be interacting with many other people from many other backgrounds, and we want to encourage everyone in this group to maintain their high level of accepted behavior regardless of what others may suggest or invite them to participate in.

3.   Drinking of alcoholic beverages by travelers under 19 years of age traveling without a parent will be allowed only if a signed consent form (Alcohol Consumption Release Form) from the parent or guardian is received by the group leaders before leaving on the trip.

4.   If, in the opinion of the coaches/group leaders, a player has been drinking excessively, (even if the player has a release form from his/her parents) playing time will be reduced at the discretion of the coaches.

5.   Drinking without an Alcohol Consumption Release Form will be a basis for immediate return of the player to the parent or guardian for the duration of the trip. If a parent/s is not on the trip, the costs of returning the player back to their home will be charged to that family.

6.   Non-TEAM SEATTLE visitors will not be allowed in the hotel rooms. Part of the great opportunity of this trip is to meet new people. Therefore, it is perfectly acceptable for players to connect with new people and make friends. But for safety and security, they may not be invited to our hotel rooms. The public areas are acceptable.

7.   Drugs, fireworks, weapons (including pellet guns), pornography, and foul or abusive language ("trash talk") will not allowed.

8.   At games, practices and related events, players will check in and out with the coaches when leaving the area of the team. At other times, "minor-aged" members will check in and out with their parent/guardian (s) when leaving their company. Guardians must know the whereabouts of their charges at all times.

9.   A buddy system is required for excursions outside the immediate area of the coaches. At games, this means 2 or more. When not at a game, 3 or more are required for excursions, AND the parent (s)/guardian (s) must have been given approval.

10.   We obviously do not expect anyone to get into trouble with the law. However, we do want to make it clear that problems with the law in a foreign country are far more severe than at home. Therefore, we need to be extra careful to abide by the rules of the society that we are visiting. Ask before touching merchandise. Do transactions in view of others. Avoid shady people, places and bargains.

11.   Personal safety for yourself and your team members is important on this trip. It is critical to recognize that the traffic rules follow different customs in different countries, and it is important to avoid being run over by a car, bicycle, or train. This may sound humorous, but the pedestrian does not have the clear right-of-way in Europe. If you step out in front of a train, the train will win. If you are standing on a curb and you are pushing or shoving for any reason, and someone gets bumped into the path of a car, the car will still win.

12.   Playing Time: We will arrange playing time to be as equitable as possible. For teams of 15 or more, we will probably set up a rotation system where certain players will not suit up for certain games. They would be free to go sightseeing, for example. We will allow people to volunteer, and then we will make assignments either by random draw, or by some other decision process. This will be determined when we have the schedules.

13.   The behavior on the field should be at the highest level. Yellow cards and red cards are the same in Europe as they are in the United States. We encourage everyone to play hard, however, keep in mind that it is a game and it is more important to have a good time on this trip than to win a game. Be aware that different cultures take soccer on a much more serious level. For example, the player from Columbia who had an own goal and was later shot when he returned to this country. It is possible that we will run into players that are taking the game far too seriously, and we need to just back away if confrontations become a possibility. Again, this applies to all TEAM SEATTLE members.

14.   If a guardian and their charges wish to deviate from a planned meal, tour or event, they are to notify the group leaders the previous day. That notice must include names, the general destination, and expected return time. Such deviations affect our busses, hotels and tours all of which require notice.

Appendix B6-b

Agreement of Behavior Form

TEAM SEATTLE
AGREEMENT OF BEHAVIOR
FOR TEAM SEATTLE MEMBERS

I _____ have read the Agreement of Behavior for Team Seattle Members and am willing to abide by its conditions. I acknowledge that as a part of the TEAM SEATTLE Travel Group that my behavior is a reflection on all of its members.

Signed(Member): _____

Date: _____

Signed(PARENT OR GUARDIAN): _____
          (if member is not 21)

*** Please sign this document and return it.
          THANK YOU.

Appendix C

Traveler Trip Detail Confirmation Form

TEAM SEATTLE 2004
TRAVELER TRIP DETAIL CONFIRMATION

The details listed below are our current record of arrangements made for the Team Seattle Travelers listed. If these are NOT correct, call Larry & Mary Kay now. *Sign below. Keep a copy for yourself, and return to us ASAP.*

TRAVELER NAME	TEAM	FLIGHTS & DEVIATIONS
1.		
2.		
3.		
4.		

Group A
SCANDINAVIAN AIRLINES (SAS)

June 25	Seattle-Copenhagen	SK 938	19.00-13.30
June 26	Copenhagen-Barcelona	JK 104	14.30-17.20
July 10	Milan-Copenhagen	SK 2682	11.00-13.05
July 10	Copenhagen-Seattle	SK 937	15.50-16.50

Group B
BRITISH AIRWAYS (BA)

June 25	Seattle-London	BA 048	18.40-12.00
June 26	London-Barcelona	BA 480	14.20-17.30
July 10	Milan-London	BA 573	12.00-13.05
July 10	London-Seattle	BA 049	14.35-16.15

Group C
NORTHWEST AIRLINES/KLM (NWKL)

June 25	Seattle-Detroit	NW 212	12.40-19.55
June 25	Detroit-Amsterdam	NW 48	21.35-11.25
June 26	Amsterdam-Barcelona	KL 1667	12.25-14.35
July 10	Bologna-Amsterdam	KL 1584	12.10-14.20
July 10	Amsterdam-Minneapolis	NW 55	16.35-18.20
July 10	Minneapolis-Seattle	NW 165	20.55-22.42

Group L
LAND-ONLY. Are arranging their own air travel. These Land-only members must arrange their flight arrival/departure times to coincide with one of our group arrival/departure times if they wish to use the bus transfer to or from the hotels and the airports. YOU MUST MAKE YOUR REQUEST TO CARRY IN ADVANCE TO SECURE THESE SEATS. ALL BUSSES MAY FILL UP.

BALANCE DUE BEFORE JUNE 1st ($100 late fee per traveler)

Member	Trip Cost	Deviation	Total Trip Cost
1.			
2.			
3.			
4.			

FINAL PAYMENT DUE $

FORMS NEED:
M = Membership. **TR** = Traveler Release. **MR** = Minor Release. **A** = Alcohol Consent. **G** = Guardianship.
P = Passport. **B** = Behavior Agreement. **C** = Coach's Agreement.
1.   2.   3.   4.

Your signature below confirms that the above information is correct for all travelers listed.

Signature X _____ Date X _____

Appendix D

Packing Information Sheet

TEAM SEATTLE SPAIN/FRANCE/ITALY 2004
Packing Information

1. Pack light. Bring clothes to allow you to layer over each other. Leave your designer clothes at home.
2. Put a copy of your passport inside all luggage. Tag your luggage on the outside with your Name, Address, City, State, Country, Zip code and Phone.
3. Use a **PINK** TEAM SEATTLE code ribbon on the handle of your luggage.
4. Remove carry straps from luggage and pack inside.
5. Remember the luggage and carry-on restrictions. You can check-in 1 bag of 70 pounds, which must each be less than 62 linear inches (length + height + width).
6. Remember the restrictions on your carry-on luggage are 45 linear inches (ex. = 22" X 14" X 9") and must weigh less than 18 pounds.

Blue ESR Tee Shirt	Bar Soap in Ziploc bag
Dryer Sheets (Bounce) in a Ziploc Bag	Granulated Detergent
(for freshening soccer bags)	(in Ziploc bag) or Sm Woolite
1-2 face wash cloths	Copy of your passport
Sun tan lotion and sun block	Insect repellant

First aid: band aids, ointment, aspirin/Tylenol, pepto tabs, prescriptions (in original prescription bottle) contact solutions, cold/allergy medications

Reading books	15' clothes line/6 clothes pins
Sun glasses	4 plastic grocery bags
Adapters/voltage regulators	Special Gifts
Money belt/Security Wallet	Camera (disposables with flash?)
Trading Items (pins, hats, t-shirts)	1 10 gal Garbage Bags
Team Seattle Travel Folder	(for dirty clothes)
Small snack bars	Sun Hat (or buy there?)
Swimming Suit	Soccer Cleats
Playing Cards/Small Games	Bags of Candy to share w/ teams

Pictures of family & Seattle to show new friends in Europe.

10 – 20 foil wrapped Moist Towelettes	Deflated Soccer Ball
Small packets of tissue	Shin Guards
Green Soccer Socks	1-2 Pair of White Soccer Socks
Sandals	Athletic Tape

PLAYERS: (Recommend that these go in your carry-on)

Green & Gray Team Seattle Jerseys	Green Team Seattle Shorts
Numbered Team Seattle Tee Shirt	Traveler's Checks/Euros/Dollars
Your Passport	Plane Ticket

Appendix E

Team Travel Tips

TEAM SEATTLE TRAVEL TIPS

TICKETS
Please check your airline tickets and verify the flight times and numbers with the information sheets in your Team Seattle Travel Folder.

AIRPORT ARRIVAL
1. **Arrive 3 hours prior to flight departure.**
2. Make sure your suitcase are **UNLOCKED**. Keep the key on you to keep case locked in hotel.
3. Make sure to tie "identifying" **PINK** Team Seattle ribbon on the suitcase handles.
4. Make sure passport copies are inside your suitcase.
5. Check in with your team leader at your airline's desk – have your passport & airline ticket out.

AIRPORT BEHAVIOR
1. Respect security and customs staff. If they delay one of us, the whole group is held up!
2. Single file – no pushing. Guardians line up just behind players.
3. NO JOKING regarding weapons, bombs, etc. Be prepared to remove your shoes, belt, etc.
4. After going through security checkpoints, collect your belongings and wait there until your group have all gone through – STAY TOGETHER. Leave only with permission from your group leader. Check in with them upon your return.
5. Do not leave your belongings unattended – they will get stolen.

AIRPORT LAYOVERS
1. Remember that you should be at your airport gate for your next flight 1 hour early. There may be changes that you should be aware of for long layovers.
2. If you decided to leave the gate areas, be aware that local ground transportation can be late and may delay your return to catch your next flight.
3. If you miss a flight, it is **your responsibility and expense** to rejoin the group.

TEAM SEATTLE BUS TRANSPORTATION
1. Busses leave at the time posted. Boarding will occur 10 minutes prior to leave time.
2. Because we do a "head count" before we leave each stop, please get on the SAME BUS YOU BOARD THAT DAY. Players load from the back forward, boosters from the front back.
3. When boarding buses, please pair up. Every seat will be needed.
4. Luggage and soccer bags will always be placed in the buses' luggage compartment below instead of carrying onto the bus, unless told otherwise by YOUR group leader.
5. Do not wear cleats or muddy shoes on the bus, or eat/drink without permission from the driver. Don't use restrooms on the bus unless approved by your group leader.
6. Teams goings to the games WILL RIDE THE SAME BUS WITH THEIR COACH.

VALUABLES
1. We discourage bringing expensive jewelry, watches, CD players etc.
2. It is your responsibility to keep your valuables protected. Use the hotel safe/room safe to store your passport, money, etc. IF THERE IS A FEE, IT IS WORTH IT! Keep your suitcase locked. For the hotel safe at their front desk, you will get a receipt. Save it.
3. Minor's passports and extra money should be given to their guardians for safekeeping.
4. Hidden money belts that are worn under "tucked in" shirts are recommended. Neck string type money holders are sometimes easily grabbed by knocking you to the ground.
5. Only carry the amount of cash that you'll need for that day's adventures.
6. Purses are an easy mark for thefts, as can cameras on your wrist.

INTRODUCTIONS
This is a very large Team Seattle group. Please make the effort to introduce yourself to members and make new friends. Our past groups said making new friends on the trip was one of the highlights.

Appendix F

Coach's Agreement Sheet

Team Seattle
COACH'S AGREEMENT

- To support the Team Seattle credo: NO WHINERS & NO PRIMA DONNAS
- To represent Team Seattle in a professional and proactive manner.
- To cooperate with Team Seattle Group Leaders, assistants, and other coaches.
- After giving your opinion, to support the decisions of the Team Seattle Group Leaders, Mary Kay and Larry French, knowing that such decisions were made with the best interests of the whole group.
- To take the member players and build a workable team.
- To assist upon request in the recruiting of additional players for Team Seattle.
- To return phone calls/emails from Group Leaders and Team Seattle members within 24 hours.
- To attend Team Seattle meetings and social events assisting in the planning, setup and teardown.
- To attend receptions given by our host Clubs and Cities.
- To set an example and arrive 5 minutes early to rendezvous for bus departures, for receptions/events, and for meals.
- To wear your Team Seattle Coaches polo at all official receptions, meetings and photo sessions.
- To schedule, organize and run 10 practices prior to the departure date. It is suggested that there be at least 2 per week the two weeks before departure.
- To be responsible for all players on your team from the time the group has gathered for a game or practice at our lodging site, through transport, warm up, play and return to the lodging site.
- To confirm with individual guardian's their role in monitoring their player's behavior on and off the field (hotels, excursions, transfers).
- To reward players with playing time based on their personal commitment at their individual skill level.
- To focus on exposing the players to the fun of playing soccer as a way to meet other international youth even if we don't win a game.
- To inform the Group Leaders and player guardians of infractions of Team Seattle rules. Major infractions include:
  - Leaving the group without notifying their guardian.
  - Traveling in groups of less than 3.
  - Having non-Team Seattle members in sleeping rooms.
  - Sneaking out alone and/or past a posted curfew.
  - Being involved in any crime that is illegal in our host nation.
  - Instigating a fight.
  - Being involved in thievery, vandalism or other destructive behavior.

SIGNATURE:_____DATE:_____

Appendix G

Recipes

Mary Kay's Seasoning Mixture

In many of the follow recipes, one of the ingredients listed will be "Mary Kay's Seasoning Mix." She had made this simple concoction for ease in cooking and also as a tool to teach new cooks some helpful short cuts.

1 cup granulated garlic

1 cup granulated onion

1/4 cup salt

1/4 cup pepper

Mix all together. Store in a sealed container as you would any dry mix.

Appendix G (continued)

GAZPACHO

Catalan Style

Each region of Spain has its signature dishes, but this chilled soup is at the top of our list from our trips to the Costa Brava. The Catalan version is different as it uses cream. The kids love this too as they get to build their own soup using the condiments. This is a wonderful treat at the end of a hot day at work. Make it a day or two ahead and enjoy it as you wish.

1 quart Spicy V-8 juice

2 slices white bread

1/4 cup olive oil

Mary Kay's Seasoning

1/2 cup cream

2 tablespoons balsamic vinegar

Condiments

Chopped red onion

Chopped red and green pepper

Chopped tomato

Chopped cucumber

Homemade croutons

Sour Cream

Olive Oil

Slice crust off bread. In large bowl, put bread slices and pour spicy V-8 juice. Leave in refrigerator for at least ½ hour or until bread gets mushy. With wire whisk, add remaining ingredients and mix until smooth. Chill until cold.

Serve gazpacho in a bowl, and let each person put the vegetable condiments first, then croutons, and pour a little bit of olive oil and last top off with sour cream.

Appendix G (continued)

HOTEL VALTORTA SAUCE

While touring with 4 teams near Florence, we stayed at a little, family-run hotel. Every morning the delivery trucks would show up at the kitchen door and we would listen to the bartering. The food was home-cooked by the relatives and we had this great sauce as part of several dinners. It is very versatile and easy to make. It is also a sauce that you don't find in restaurants or in many cookbooks, so it is special enough for company too.

2 cups sliced mushrooms

3-4 garlic cloves sliced

2-4 tablespoons olive oil

2 tablespoons butter

3 tablespoons flour

1/2 cup beef broth

1/2 cup whipping cream

1/2 cup red wine

1 jar pitted Kalamata olives (drained)

Salt & pepper

Kitchen Bouquet (for color)

Saute mushrooms and garlic in olive oil and butter until garlic turns slightly brown. Add flour, stir with wire whisk until smooth, then add beef broth, red wine and cream keep stirring to prevent lumps. Add a little Kitchen Bouquet for color. Simmer to reduce sauce until thick. Add olives.

4 servings – good on chicken, pork, or veal.

Appendix G (continued)

BOEUF BOURGUIGNON
Beef Burgundy

The food in France is always amazing. We had this mouth-watering treat at a little café' deep in the heart of old Nice on the French Riviera. As Nice is a seaside city, we were surprised as the variety of "non-seafood" entrees throughout this area. This is a simple meal, but will be a hit with family and friends.

Bon Appetit!!!

2 1/2 lbs. beef chuck roast cubed
2 tablespoon olive oil
1 lb carrots sliced diagonally in 1" cubes
1 yellow onion sliced
6 slices bacon, diced
2 cloves garlic diced
1 bottle red wine
1 can beef broth
1 tablespoons tomato paste
1 teaspoon thyme
1/3 stick butter
3 tablespoons flour
1 bag frozen baby onions
1 lb sliced mushrooms
Mary Kay's seasoning
Salt & fresh ground pepper

In a stew pot, heat olive oil. Add the bacon and cook over medium heat for 10 minutes until bacon is lightly brown. Remove the bacon with a slotted spoon to a large plate.

Season the beef with salt and pepper. In batches, sear the beef in the bacon drippings & olive oil. Remove sear cubes to the plate with the bacon and continue searing until all beef is browned. Set aside.

Sauté the carrot and onions in the same pan for 10 minutes or until onions are slightly brown. Add garlic and cook for 1 more minute. Put the meat and bacon back into the pot with any juices that have accumulated on the plate. Add wine and beef broth. Add tomato paste, thyme, and Mary Kay's seasoning. Bring to a boil, cover the pot with a tight-fitting lid, and place in the oven for about 1 hour, or until the meat is tender. Remove from the oven and put on the stove.

Combine 2 tablespoons of the butter and the flour with a fork and stir into the stew. Add frozen onions. In medium plan, sauté the mushrooms in the remaining butter for 10 minutes or until lightly brown, and then add to the stew. Bring the stew to a boil, then lower the heat and simmer uncovered for 15 minutes.

Appendix G (continued)

VEAL SALTIMBOCCA

Some recipes are just staples with every region. For Italy, veal saltimbocca is one of them. We have had this in Verona in northern Italy and all the way down to Sorrento near Naples.

This is also a good recipe to include kids and new aspiring cooks. It gives them a hands on chance to create something that sounds very difficult, but isn't. And the rewards are in the eating and in the compliments.

6 Veal scallopini filets

Mary Kay's seasoning

Salt and pepper

Flour for dredging

2 Tablespoons butter

4 Tablespoons olive oil

1 cup white wine

6 slices prosciutto

6 slices mozzarella

Season the veal with salt and pepper.

Dredge the veal in seasoned flour (using Mary Kay's seasoning).

In a large sauté pan, over medium heat, melt butter and olive oil and sauté veal until cooked.

Take veal out and place into a Pyrex pan and top with mozzarella first, and then put prosciutto on top of the cheese.

Add wine to the pan to make the sauce and simmer until thick

Bake 350 degrees until the cheese melts.

Put the sauce on a plate first and then the veal.

Add your favorite pasta and grilled vegetables to the plate and you are set!

Appendix G (continued)

SESAME CRUNCHY CHICKEN WINGS

Although this recipe has nothing to do with our soccer travels, it is a recipe that Mary Kay adapted from Hawaiian sources. It is a bit time consuming and you want to keep the kitchen windows open while doing the frying, but it is the number one most requested of all of Mary Kay's many great recipes. Most family and friends just refer to it at "crunchy chicken".

Kids love this at birthday parties. It is a hit at adult hors d'oeuvre parties, and we have used it at many of our soccer pot lucks. What more is there in life that family, friends, good health and good food!!

3 lbs. chicken wings

8 Tablespoons cornstarch

4 Tablespoons flour

4 Tablespoons sugar

2 Tablespoons granulated garlic

1 1/2 teaspoons salt

5 Tablespoons soy sauce

2 eggs

2 Tablespoons sesame seed

2 stalks green onion chopped

- Measure dry ingredients in a large bowl.
- Add eggs, soy sauce and green onions.
- Add chicken wings and make sure chicken gets coated.
- Marinate overnight.
- Fry chicken wings until golden brown.

Appendix G (continued)

DUTCH BABY PANCAKES

Holland, The Netherlands is one of our favorite countries. Our soccer adventures there showed us that some of our favorite breakfast foods like waffles came from that region.

These Dutch Baby Pancakes are very versatile and can be fun for the family breakfast or for brunch with friends. Letting guests select their favorite fruit toppings is a nice touch.

At the bottom of this page, it is mentioned that you can put this recipe in muffin tins for kids. Our sons, Brent and Adam, named these "UGLY PUFFS" as the shapes come out contorted, but again, the kids love filling their "ugly puff" cups with everything from fruit to M & M's.

Preheat oven to 425 degrees

1/2 cup flour
1/2 cup milk
2 eggs
1/4 stick butter
Lemon juice
Powdered sugar

Put butter into a pie pan and melt in the oven.

Beat eggs with wire whisk in medium bowl. Add flour and milk and mix until smooth. When butter is melted, add egg mixture. Bake about 20-30 minutes until batter starts to rise and turns brown (sides will rise more than the middle). Open the oven and squeeze fresh lemon juice and sprinkle with powder sugar (immediately the pancake middle will sink. Put back in the oven for a few minutes.

Serve with whipped cream and fruit (especially strawberries, blueberries) or can be eaten plain.

For children:

Put the batter in muffins tins. Put a little pat of butter in each muffin hole and melt in the oven. Pour batter in each muffin hole at least half full. Bake 15 minutes or until batter turns brown and looks like a popover. Remove mini pancakes on to a cookie sheet and sprinkle with powder sugar. When the pancake cools, the middle sinks and they look like a cup. So we filled them with fruit and whipped cream.

Appendix G (continued)

CRÈME BRULEE

When we look at menus or plan a dinner party, we always begin with the dessert and work backwards. This recipe has counterparts in Spain, France and Italy and is one of our favorites. And if you are going to break away from your doctor's "food rules" for a meal, this is one to do it for!

3 cups whipping cream

4 eggs yolks

1 whole egg

1/2 cup sugar

1 teaspoon vanilla extract

2 tablespoons Grand Marnier

Preheat oven to 350 degrees

Take Kitchen Aid with paddle attachment, beat eggs and sugar together on low speed until just combined. Meanwhile, scald the cream in small saucepan until very hot to touch, but not boiled.

With the mixer on low speed, slowly add the cream to the egg mixture. Add the vanilla and Grand Marnier and pour into ramekins until almost full.

Place ramekins in a baking pan and carefully pour boiling water into the pan to come halfway up the sides of the ramekins. Bake for 35 to 40 minutes, until the custards are set. Remove the custards from the water bath, cool to room temperature, and refrigerate until firm.

To serve, spread 1 tablespoon of sugar evenly on the top of each ramekins and heat with a kitchen blowtorch until the sugar caramelizes evenly (can be done under a broiler as well).

Appendix G (continued)

TIRAMISU

Everyone who knows Italy or who likes sweets knows tiramisu. Mary Kay's adaptation of this traditional favorite takes you right to Venice. Although there are a few steps involved, it is worth the effort. This can surprisingly feed a lot of people as it is very rich.

2 packages ladyfingers (dry)

2 1/2 cups hot water

1/4 cup sugar

5 teaspoons instant espresso powder + 1 tablespoon

1/4 cup brandy

2 tablespoons vanilla extract

2-8 oz. containers of mascarpone cheese

1/4 cup powdered sugar

2 cups whipping cream

1 tablespoon cocoa powder

Cover bottom of 13 x 9 x 2 inch glass baking dish with single layer of ladyfingers. Combine water, sugar and espresso powder in a large bowl and stir until sugar and espresso powder dissolves. Stir in brandy and vanilla. Pour 1 cup espresso mixture over ladyfingers in the baking dish. Reserve remaining espresso mixture.

Beat mascarpone and 1/8 cup powdered sugar with Kitchen Aid or electric mixer until creamy. In another bowl, beat the whipping cream with Kitchen Aid or electric mixer. Fold in ½ of the beaten whipped cream in the mascarpone mixture (save the remaining whipped cream for later). Spread the mascarpone mixture over the soaked ladyfingers. Then arrange ladyfingers over the mascarpone mixture and carefully pour the espresso mixture over the second layer of ladyfingers.

In small bowl, add the rest of the powdered sugar and 1 tablespoon cocoa powder and 1 tablespoon espresso and stir until mixed. Fold this mixture into the remaining whipped cream and spread over the second layer of ladyfingers.

Garnish with chocolate–coated coffee beans

Appendix G (continued)

HAWAIIAN BREAKFAST COOKIES

This recipe is included as it is a hallmark at our orientation meetings. Getting prospective members together is always easier with warm cookies. We will be traveling with these people and want them to relax and be comfortable with us. Sharing these great cookies is a great "ice breaker." And of course, we make them anytime for our family to enjoy as well.

1 cup butter, softened

1 cup firmly packed brown sugar

1/2 cup granulated sugar

2 eggs

1 tsp. Vanilla

1 1/2 cup flour

2 tsp. baking soda

1/2 tsp. Salt

3 cups oatmeal

2 cups cornflakes

1/2 cup shredded coconut

1-11 oz. package white chocolate chips

1 cup chopped macadamia nuts (optional)

Pre–heat oven to 350 degrees.

Beat butter, sugars until creamy. Add eggs and vanilla. Sift together flour, baking soda, and salt. Slowly add to butter mixture. Then add cornflakes, coconut, nuts. Make balls and press on cookie sheet. Bake 10-12 minutes until golden brown.

Appendix G (continued)

ARTICHOKE DIP

This is another of those great, easy standby recipes that can fill many "emergency" situations. Whether it is served at a group potluck during a team meeting, or for a "grown up" party, everyone always makes a big deal over it. Kids of all ages love it. You can offer it with tortilla chips, crackers or bread as you wish. There will rarely be anything left!!

1 block cream cheese

1/2-cup mayonnaise

1 can crab (with juice)

1 can quarter artichoke hearts

1 tablespoon Worcestershire sauce

1/2-cup shredded cheddar cheese

Mary Kay's seasoning

Soften cream cheese in microwave about 20 seconds. In a bowl, mash cream cheese with fork. Add mayonnaise and stir until creamy. Chop artichokes and add to cream cheese mixture. Add rest of the ingredients. Put dip in casserole dish and bake 350 degrees approximately 30 minutes. Serve hot with crackers and French bread.

Appendix G (continued)

TACO SOUP

Although this is not an "international" discovery, this recipe has made cameo appearances at dozens of our all-team meetings, end of season parties and when hosting out of town teams in exchanges. We have distributed this recipe to members who show up at the event with their pots full of hot Taco Soup ready to feed the hungry masses. It is so easy that we've had the players make the soup as well. It is also a meal that can be made a day or two in advance, cooled in your frig in shallow, uncovered pans, then reheated at needed (we've even broken out the camp stove to reheat this at soccer field. Enjoy!!!

1 1/2 lbs ground beef

1 small yellow onion chopped

1 (28 oz) can diced tomatoes with juice

1 (14 oz) can kidney beans

1 (17 oz) can corn with juice

1 (8 oz) can tomato sauce

1 cup water

1 package taco seasoning

TOPPINGS

Shredded cheddar cheese

Fritos

Sour cream

Chopped Green Onions

Brown meat in a large pot and add onions. Cook until onions are tender. Add remaining ingredients and simmer 60 minutes.

Pour soup into a bowl and have each person add the toppings as desired.

(feeds 6 to 8)